MASSACHUSETTS

OFF THE BEATEN PATH®

EIGHTH EDITION

MASSACHUSETTS

OFF THE BEATEN PATH®

DISCOVER YOUR FUN

MARIA OLIA

Globe
Pequot

Essex, Connecticut

All the information in this guidebook is subject to change. We recommend that you call ahead to obtain current information before traveling.

Globe Pequot

An imprint of Globe Pequot, the trade division of
The Rowman & Littlefield Publishing Group, Inc.
4501 Forbes Blvd., Ste. 200
Lanham, MD 20706
www.rowman.com

Distributed by NATIONAL BOOK NETWORK

British Library Cataloguing in Publication Information available

Library of Congress Cataloging-in-Publication Data: This title is a serial and is covered under LCCN 2002207390.

ISBN 9781493070480 (paperback) | ISBN 9781493070497 (ebook)

♾™ The paper used in this publication meets the minimum requirements of American National Standard for Information Sciences—Permanence of Paper for Printed Library Materials, ANSI/NISO Z39.48-1992.

Contents

Acknowledgments vi

About the Author vii

Introduction ix

Greater Boston **1**

North of Boston **33**

South of Boston **52**

Cape Cod **64**

Worcester County **91**

Pioneer Valley **105**

The Berkshires **119**

Index 133

Acknowledgments

For those of us lucky enough to live in Massachusetts, it is a fantastic place to call home. Writing *Massachusetts Off the Beaten Path* has been a dream assignment.

This book is dedicated to my family. I am indebted to my parents, Robert and Josephine Dascanio, for encouraging my travels as a young girl. As always, I am grateful to my supportive and enthusiastic children and their families: Bijan, Ellie and Maya; Kian and Alicia; Cameron and Leda. And finally, many thanks to my husband, Masoud, my lifelong travel partner, for sharing the journey.

About the Author

A near-native New Englander, **Maria Olia** is a freelance writer who has lived in Newton, just outside of Boston, for more than thirty years. Her work has appeared in the *Boston Globe, National Geographic, Mobil Travel,* and *Working Mother* magazine. She is the author of seven books, including *No Access Boston* and *Day Trips New England* (Globe Pequot Press). Catch up with Maria at mariaolia.com.

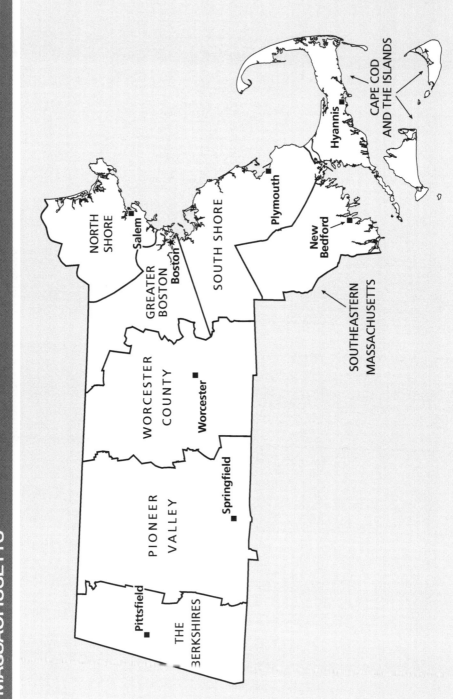

MASSACHUSETTS

NORTH SHORE

Salem ■

GREATER BOSTON

★ Boston

SOUTH SHORE

Plymouth ■

New Bedford ■

SOUTHEASTERN MASSACHUSETTS

Hyannis ■

CAPE COD AND THE ISLANDS

WORCESTER COUNTY

Worcester ■

PIONEER VALLEY

Springfield ■

THE BERKSHIRES

Pittsfield ■

Introduction

Tucked into the northeast corner of the United States, Massachusetts is known as the Bay State because of its wide Atlantic gulf enclosed by the hooked peninsula of Cape Cod. Massachusetts is the name of the native tribe that lived near the bay and means "at the great hill."

Some four-hundred-plus years ago, the Puritans arrived, and that hill became Boston: "We shall be as a city upon a hill; the eyes of all people are upon us." By the 1720s the city had developed around the harbor, becoming the capital of Massachusetts Bay Colony and the hub of New England. It still is.

Massachusetts has more than a little history; from Boston to the Berkshires, Massachusetts preserves its past like no other. As you explore Massachusetts's main streets and back roads, you'll discover that nearly every town has its share of sites—historic markers, house museums, as well as parks and open spaces that offer a window to the past.

But Massachusetts is much more than history. Can you know a country and understand its people through its authors? Some of America's most important early writers who helped in developing an American viewpoint and voice—Longfellow, Thoreau, Melville, and Dickinson, among others—have called Massachusetts home.

The Bay State has miles of coastline and spectacular beaches, each more memorable than the last. Head west to the forested mountains of the Berkshire hills for outdoor pursuits both summer and winter, with the rich farmland of the Pioneer Valley in between.

Tourists rarely travel west from the urban center of Boston and Cape Cod's beaches. But if you don't get off that well-trodden path every now and then, you can miss some of the very best that Massachusetts has to offer.

This book is also about some of Massachusetts's most intriguing and lesser-known spots. In these pages you'll find recommendations for what to do, what to see, where to eat, where to stay and what not to miss. Some places are not off the beaten path; they are, in fact, hidden in plain sight. Massachusetts also has an abundance of opportunities for quieter moments if you know where to look—places to hike, bike, and paddle. All are worth going out of the way to experience.

Chances are that a single trip to Massachusetts won't be enough. Fortunately, the state is a wonderful destination to return to again and again. You'll likely be back.

Disclaimer: Over the last couple of years, many establishments have modified their hours and or operations in response to the COVID-19 pandemic. It's always a good idea to check for the latest information before heading out.

Massachusetts Facts

Nickname: The Bay State. People who hail from Massachusetts are known as "Bay Staters."

Capital: Boston

Population: 7,033,469, 15th in the country

Area: 10,565 square miles, 44th in the country

Admitted to the Union: Massachusetts became the 6th state when it was admitted on February 6, 1788.

Major Cities: Boston, population 696,959; Worcester, 185,047; Springfield, 151,437; Cambridge, 121,255; Lowell, 109,902; Brockton, 95,663; New Bedford, 95,339; Quincy, 94,671; Newton, 87,733

Famous People Born in Massachusetts: Benjamin Franklin, Paul Revere, John Hancock, President John Adams, President John Quincy Adams, Susan B. Anthony, Edgar Allan Poe, Theodor Seuss Geisel, N. C. Wyeth, Bette Davis, President John F. Kennedy, Leonard Bernstein, President George H. W. Bush, Malcolm X, Leonard Nimoy, Kurt Russell, Michael Bloomberg, Mike Wallace, Lesley Stahl, Matthew Perry, Matt LeBlanc, Uma Thurman, Amy Poehler, Mark Wahlberg, Conan O'Brien, Matt Damon, Steve Carell, Chris Evans, John Krasinski, B. J. Novak, Mindy Kaling

Current Famous Residents: President Barack and Michelle Obama (Martha's Vineyard), Celeste Ng, Ibram X. Kendi, Yo-Yo Ma, John Malkovich, Ted Danson and Mary Steenburgen (Martha's Vineyard), Carly Simon (Martha's Vineyard), James Taylor, Steve Carell, Spike Lee (Martha's Vineyard), Steven Tyler, Harry Connick Jr., Dan Aykroyd (Martha's Vineyard), Chris Cooper

Travel Information: The Massachusetts Office of Travel and Tourism site is Visit Massachusetts (136 Blackstone St., Boston 02109; 617-973-8500; visitma .com). Find trip planning ideas and resources including downloadable regional travel guides. The state also has a free, easy-to-use travel app that has ready-made itineraries and a tool to create your own journey.

State Parks: The Massachusetts Department of Conservation and Recreation (DCR) is the agency tasked with managing the state's more than 150 parks. Contact DCR at 251 Causeway St., Boston 02114; (617) 626-1250; mass.gov/dcr.

Major Newspapers: *Boston Globe, Boston Herald, Patriot Ledger, Eagle-Tribune, Lowell Sun, Cape Cod Times, Berkshire Eagle, Worcester Telegram*

Public Transportation: Massachusetts's major regional air center is Boston Logan International Airport (BOS) located in East Boston—just 3 miles from downtown. More than fifty domestic and international carriers fly out of Logan. Logan is a hub for both JetBlue (800-530-2583; jetblue.com) and Delta (800-221-1212; delta.com). Amtrak (800-872-7245; amtrak.com) has ten stations in Massachusetts, including three in Boston. Regional bus service is plentiful throughout the state. Principal motorcoach companies include Peter Pan (800-343-9999; peterpanbus.com), Greyhound (800-231-2222; greyhound.com), and Megabus (877-402-6342; megabus.com). The state is well served by the Massachusetts Bay Transportation Authority, known as the MBTA (mbta.com; 617-222-3200), which operates the subway system as well as the commuter rail that connects Boston to the outlying suburbs.

Climate: Massachusetts is a four-season destination, with a climate that is highly variable. Summers are usually warm but comfortable. Boston averages fourteen days with temperatures in the 90s; an occasional day with temperatures in the triple digits is not unheard of. In summer the Cape is usually cooler than Boston and inland, but the humidity is much higher. Fall brings temperate weather throughout the state, with mild days and cool nights. The result? Stunning autumn foliage. Winters in Massachusetts are notoriously cold and snowy. Average temperatures average well below freezing both day and night in January and February. Arctic air can bring bitter cold snaps and subzero temperatures. Boston's average winter snowfall is forty inches, while Worcester's average total snowfall is sixty-five inches. And spring? Since March is still wintery and April is mud season, spring in Massachusetts is the month of May.

Greater Boston

Boston is a great place to start exploring Massachusetts whether you are a local and have been here for a few generations or are visiting for the very first time. Cambridge, famously the home of Harvard University, is just across the Charles River and is a major draw for visitors from around the world for its museums and all-around cool intellectual vibe. The town of Brookline is trolley-stop distance from Boston. The birthplace of John F. Kennedy, a National Historic Site, is here, and the city has a bona fide dining scene with a large number of ethnic eateries. Just a short twenty-mile drive from Boston are the neighboring towns of Lexington and Concord, where colonists first rebelled against the British in the earliest military clash of the Revolutionary War. Next door, rural Lincoln has a somewhat surprising number of worthwhile attractions, including the DeCordova Sculpture Park and Museum, Gropius House, and Drumlin Farm, the headquarters of the Massachusetts Audubon Society.

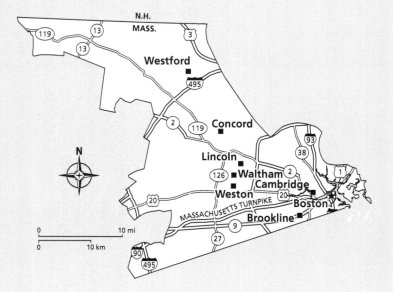

Boston

The massive, once-in-a-lifetime Central Artery Project, known as the "Big Dig," dramatically changed Boston's skyline. The elevated portion of Interstate 93, which cut off downtown from the waterfront, is no more; the gridlock that used to plague the ride to and from Logan Airport has virtually disappeared; and the city gained an instant landmark with the sweeping, cable-stayed Zakim Bridge.

What emerged from nearly fifteen years of development and $24 billion is the newly fabulous Seaport District, along with three hundred acres of new parks and open space. The project reconnected the city physically and psychologically with the waterfront. Boston has never looked better.

AUTHOR'S TOP TEN PICKS

Arnold Arboretum
125 The Arborway
Boston
(617) 524-1718
arboretum.harvard.edu

Battle Road Trail at Minuteman National Park
250 N. Great Rd.
Lincoln
(781) 674-1920
nps.gov/mima

Boston Harbor Islands
191 W. Atlantic Ave.
Boston
(617) 227-4321
bostonharborislands.com

DeCordova Sculpture Park & Museum
51 Sandy Pond Rd.
Lincoln
(781) 259-8355
decordova.org

Freedom Trail
139 Tremont St.
Boston
(617) 3577-8300
thefreedomtrail.org

Harvard Museum of Natural History
26 Oxford St.
Cambridge
(617) 495-3045
hmnh.harvard.edu

Isabella Stewart Gardner Museum
25 Evans Way
Boston
(617) 566-4101
gardnermuseum.org

Metropolitan Waterworks Museum
2450 Beacon St.
Boston
(617) 277-0065
waterworksmuseum.org

Mount Auburn Cemetery
580 Mount Auburn St.
Cambridge
(617) 547-7105
mountauburn.org

Museum of African American History
46 Joy St.
Boston
(617) 725-0022
maah.org

Off the Beaten Path: The Freedom Trail Edit

Hear, ye, hear ye. In case you haven't heard, Boston is just a little bit important regarding the whole American Revolution thing. The two-and-a-half-mile redbrick pedestrian path (in some places it's painted) that wends itself through the heart of downtown Boston is one of America's finest open-air museums and includes places known by every American history buff, including the Boston Massacre, Paul Revere House, and the USS *Constitution*.

Yes, the Freedom Trail is a literal tourist trail—you are certainly not charting unknown terrain here. But you can't help but feel moved by history as you walk in the footsteps of the colonists who, by the 1760s, helped to make Boston the hotbed of resistance to British authority in America.

Most visitors will begin tracing the route from the Meet Boston information center at the Boston Common (139 Tremont St.) and dutifully walk to visit each of the sixteen historic sites in the usual order—counting the Boston Common as the first stop and then moving on to the Massachusetts State House, Park Street Church, Granary Burying Ground (with the graves of Paul Revere, John Hancock, and Sam Adams), King's Chapel and its burying ground, the Benjamin Franklin statue and site of the country's first public school, the Old Corner Bookstore (sadly, now a Chipotle), the Old State House, the Boston Massacre site, the Old South Meeting House, Faneuil Hall, Old North Church, and the Paul Revere House; finishing in Charlestown at the USS *Constitution* and the Bunker Hill Monument at the end of one very long day. Whew!

But who says you need to do the Freedom Trail in order? Or that you even must do the trail in its entirety? You can start the trail at any point along the way and hop on and off the trail as you please. Guided tours normally cover the walk-by sites and are a great way to cover an impressive amount of ground. **Freedom Trail Foundation** (thefreedomtrail .org) guides are dressed in eighteenth-century garb and are a familiar sight on Boston's downtown streets; guides wearing the broad-brimmed ranger hats of the **National Park Service** (nps.gov/bost) are nearly as ubiquitous. Freedom Foundation tours are offered year-round; current ticket prices are $16 for adults and $8 for children. National Park Service tours are only offered seasonally, but they are free.

Anyone with a map or an app can follow the trail themselves. And the best advice is to do the Freedom Trail in reverse.

Begin your exploration in Charlestown with the **Bunker Hill Monument** and a stunning view of Boston and the harbor. This is your first stop, so you can climb the 294 steps to the top of the granite obelisk on fresh legs. The cornerstone was set in 1825 by Revolutionary War hero the Marquis de Lafayette on the fiftieth anniversary of the Battle of Bunker Hill (which actually happened on nearby Breed's Hill). Next up? Walk down to the water to board the **USS** Constitution; the three-masted wooden hull frigate stands tall and proud at her berth in the Charlestown Navy Yard. She is a beauty. Launched in 1797 (her construction was authorized by George Washington), she is the world's oldest commissioned warship still afloat. The USS *Constitution* is still a US Navy ship; thirty-minute guided tours are given on the half hour by young active-duty sailors—it's very much considered a plum assignment. Public tours are free and take place Tuesday through Sunday 10 a.m. to 5 p.m. Check tour days and hours during winter. Also leave time for security screening—adults over age eighteen must show a government-issued ID.

The longest section of the Freedom Trail is the one-mile walk across the Charlestown Bridge that spans the Charles River before depositing walkers into the North End, Boston's Italian enclave. Here you can seesaw from pizzeria to café to gelateria as you meander through the warren of narrow streets.

Having refueled, you may want to prioritize among the remaining Freedom Trail sites. Staying in the North End, you can pop into the *Paul Revere House* (617-523-2338; paulreverehouse.org) at 19 North Square. The small, gray clapboard building dates from 1680, making it one of the oldest residential homes in the city. Revere lived here with his family at the time of his fabled 1775 ride. Hours are daily 10 a.m. to 5:15 p.m. Admission is $6 adults and $1 for children. Continuing with the Revere theme, **Old North Church** (781-352-2069; oldnorth.com), of "one if by land, two if by sea" fame, is around the corner at 93 Salem Street. Sexton Robert Newman hung two lanterns in the belfry of Christ Church (as it was then known) to signal to Revere and the colonists that the British were approaching Concord by sea. Visiting hours at Old North Church are Tuesday through Saturday from 10 a.m. to 5 p.m. and Sunday 12:30 to 5 p.m. Admission is $5.

Cut across the Rose Kennedy Greenway toward shamelessly touristy *Faneuil Hall*. From here the trail becomes a lot busier, with office workers and general city hustle. Nearby, at the top of Congress Street, find the **Old State House**. It's easy to spot. Incongruously set amid modern office skyscrapers, the 1713 brick meeting house is topped with two golden statues—a lion and a unicorn (the symbols of England and Scotland)—and is the oldest public building in Boston.

In front of the Old State House, a circle of cobblestones marks the spot where a snowball fight went bad, later becoming known as the **Boston Massacre**. On March 5, 1770, what began as a brawl between a mob of rowdy colonists and a few British soldiers escalated, killing five Bostonians and wounding several others.

From here, what remains is a sweeping L-shaped walk that takes in the cluster of sites at Downtown Crossing (**Old Corner Bookstore**, **Benjamin Franklin statue** and site of the first public school, **King's Chapel and Burying Ground**, the **Granary Burying Ground**). You'll eventually end up at the **Boston Common** and the golden dome of the **Massachusetts State House**.

Yet, despite all the building and construction, Boston is still small enough to walk—and walk you shall. Visitors come to Boston, in part, to travel back in time. You can tread on the very same centuries-old cobblestone streets the Founding Fathers walked, where the drama of the American Revolution is retold to legions of tourists every day.

But the city is a lot more than sleepy colonial history. The yearly influx of 250,000 students every September and a thriving technology sector keep the city lively, diverse, and relevant. Boston is truly a world-class city, home to museums of every category as well as a big-time arts scene and dining that has finally (!) hit its culinary stride.

Faneuil Hall and its *Quincy Market* Food Court have been the unofficial pit stop for Freedom Trail visitors for seemingly forever. But just two blocks away, tucked between the Rose Fitzgerald Greenway and the Haymarket T stop, is the newer (since 2015) *Boston Public Market* (617-973-4909; bostonpublicmarket.org), which features an artisanal food hall with a focus on all things New England. Among the more than two dozen vendors that have set up shop are legendary seafood purveyor Red's Best (go for the lobster roll), cult coffeehouse *George Howell*, and small-batch ice cream maker *Crescent Ridge Farms*. Bonus: The vendors are very happy to talk about the New England food scene. The Boston Public Market is located at 100 Hanover Street; hours are Monday through Saturday 8 a.m. to 6 p.m., Sunday 10 a.m. to 6 p.m.

trivia

The peal of bells from the belfry of Old North Church fills the air of the North End every Sunday—just as it did more than three hundred years ago, when a fifteen-year-old Paul Revere was a bell ringer. Revere's connection to bells and bell ringing was lifelong; he eventually established a foundry that specialized in bell casting, producing nearly four hundred bells of all sizes for churches, ships, and schools.

Venture just steps off the Freedom Trail to reflect on freedom as it relates to more recent world events at the *New England Holocaust Memorial* (617-457-8500; nehm.org). Rising fifty-four feet skyward, six glass towers are etched with rows of seven-digit numbers, representing the tattoos of the six million Jews killed by Nazi Germany during World War II. Smoke rises from a grate beneath the illuminated towers as visitors walk along the granite path, under and through the sculptural chambers. The memorial is in Carmen Park at 98 Union Street and is open twenty-four hours; it is especially poignant in the evening.

The most photographed spot in Boston is very much "off the beaten path," but it certainly does not deter hordes of picture-taking tourists from descending on Beacon Hill's tiny *Acorn Street* daily. The pedestrian-only cobblestone lane

The Inner Harbor Ferry

The gentle sway of the sea, salt-tinged breeze, and views of the Boston skyline. Taking the **MBTA's Inner Harbor Ferry** across Boston Harbor is an extremely practical choice for visiting the USS *Constitution* and the Bunker Hill Monument. The ten-minute ride between Long Wharf (next to the Marriott Hotel) and the Charlestown Navy Yard runs daily, every thirty minutes; one-way fares are just $3.70.

boasts gas lanterns and seasonal window boxes and is lined with Federal-era brick townhomes. It's undeniably a romanticized version of colonial-era Boston—and clearly everyone is here for it.

Boston's history is more than the Freedom Trail. It is no accident that the **Shaw Memorial to the 54th Regiment** is located on the Boston Common, opposite the State House. The high-relief bronze by sculptor Augustus Saint-Gaudens dates from 1884 and is considered his masterwork; it honors Colonel Robert Gould Shaw, on horseback, leading the first African American combat unit to fight in the Civil War.

Boston, and particularly Beacon Hill, was a hotbed of antislavery sentiment in the first half of the nineteenth century. Massachusetts abolished slavery in 1783, and the north slope of Beacon Hill was home to a significant free Black community.

The Shaw Memorial is the starting point for the National Park Service's **Black Heritage Trail**, a 1.6-mile walking tour through Beacon Hill that explores ten stops that bear witness to the abolitionist debate and the hiding of fugitive slaves that took place here in the years preceding the Civil War.

Like the Freedom Trail, the Black Heritage Trail can be self-guided (pick up a map at the NPS Visitor Center at Faneuil Hall or download a trail map from the NPS website). Park ranger–led tours are offered all year (except winter) and are free. Check the NPS website for times.

The Shaw Memorial also serves as a metaphorical bridge between the Freedom Trail and the **Museum of African American History** (617-725-0022; maah.org), which is nearby at 46 Joy Street on Beacon Hill. The visitor center is located at the **African Meeting House**. Built in 1806 by the Black community, it is a sanctuary of elegant simplicity. It became known as the "Black Faneuil Hall," as it was the center of the neighborhood life; it was a place of worship, a school, and a gathering place to protest slavery. In 1832 William Lloyd Garrison founded the New England Anti-Slavery Society here. It was also here that Frederick Douglass recruited men for the newly formed 54th Regiment. Next door, the **Abiel Smith School** opened in 1835 as the first public school

trivia

During the War of 1812 and the battle between the USS *Constitution* and HMS *Guerriere* off the coast of Halifax, Nova Scotia, in the North Atlantic, British cannonballs were said to have bounced off Constitution's oak hull. The story goes that a sailor exclaimed, "Huzzah, her sides are made of iron," and she has been known as "Old Ironsides" ever since.

for Black children. Today, the African Meeting House and Abiel Smith School continue to serve their original purpose as places of assembly and public education. Admission to the museum is $10 for adults, $8 for students and seniors, and free for children age twelve and under.

No lit-minded visitor would consider a trip to Boston complete until they have browsed the antiquarian and used books at the **Brattle Book Shop** (617-542-0210; brattlebookshop.com), located at 9 West Street in Downtown Crossing. Established in 1825, the shop is owned by Ken Gloss, who is known to millions for his work as a book appraiser on PBS's *Antiques Roadshow*. The three-story shop has a delightfully old-timey feel and features more than 250,000 items in its expansive collection. These days, the shop is Instagram famous for its outdoor book lot of $1, $3, and $5 titles, all presided over by a street art mural featuring Mark Twain, Toni Morrison, and Dr. Seuss.

Just north of Beacon Hill is Boston's West End neighborhood, dominated by Massachusetts General Hospital (MGH) at 54 Fruit Street, the country's third-oldest hospital. One of the most pivotal moments in the long history of medicine occurred here on October 16, 1846, when Dr. William T. G. Morton and Dr. John Collins Warren successfully trialed anesthesia during a medical procedure to remove a tumor from a patient's neck. The operation took place in the hospital's original 1821 Charles Bulfinch–designed amphitheater. The operating theater featured tiered seating and a distinctive cupola with windows that let in abundant natural light. The Ether Dome (617-724-9557; massgeneral .org), as it is now known, has been beautifully preserved as an architectural, medical, and historical landmark and is well worth a visit by anyone with even a casual interest in medicine.

There is a cabinet-of-curiosities feeling here, with glass cases presenting an array of antique anesthetic devices—mostly of the scary and pointy variety. Similarly, in the nineteenth century, mummies were considered medical oddities. Padihersherf is a 2,500-year-old Egyptian mummy and is undoubtedly MGH's most famous resident, a gift to the city of Boston from a Dutch merchant in 1823. One of the first mummies imported to America, "Padi" was used by the young hospital as a fundraiser; people paid 25 cents each to view him.

The Ether Dome is located on the fourth floor of the Bulfinch Building. Ask for directions at the Information Desk, and you will be handed a map to navigate the hospital corridors to find the correct elevator. The Ether Dome is closed to the public when it is being used as a classroom or for meetings but is generally open to the public Monday through Friday from 9 a.m. to 5 p.m. Admission is free.

Boston Harbor Islands (617-227-4321; bostonharborislands.com). A system of trusty passenger ferries affords visitors the opportunity to explore places that few (even among native Bostonians) realize are open. Just a stone's throw from the city, there are thirty-four islands that make up the Boston Harbor Islands National State Park; six of them are accessible by ferry. The most popular island is Spectacle, which is just a thirty-minute ride away and has one of the region's best little-known swimming beaches (it's a good spot to hunt for sea glass). Another option is taking a forty-minute boat ride to George's Island, the jewel of the park and home to Fort Warren, a Civil War–era fort. A favorite park ranger tale is the legend of the "Lady in Black," said to be Mrs. Andrew Lanier, the wife of a Confederate soldier that some say still haunts the island. Along with guided tours, George's offers walking trails, picnic facilities, and captivating views from Adirondack chairs that look out to the harbor. Another possibility is booking a two-hour narrated lighthouse cruises (seasonal; weekends only). You will see the lighthouses as sailors do—from the water (sadly, no disembarking)—and pass three lighthouses, including Boston Light. Dating from 1716, it is the first and oldest lighthouse in the country. Both Spectacle and George's have concession stands, although many visitors choose to bring a picnic lunch from Faneuil Hall or the Public Market vendors. The Boston Harbor Islands Welcome Center is on the Rose Kennedy Greenway at 191 West Atlantic Avenue, next to the ***Greenway Carousel***. And since one is never too old or too young to ride a carousel, this is your chance. Rides are just $4.

Still in downtown, you'll find that for a seafood shack, ***James Hook Lobster*** (617-423-5501; jameshooklobster.com) has prime harborside real estate, which means you can enjoy that hot, buttered lobster roll and creamy clam chowder on the water against a stunning backdrop of city views. Located close to the Seaport District at 44 Atlantic Avenue, Hook's has picnic tables and limited indoor seating; there's beer and wine too.

Practically next door, at 470 Atlantic Avenue, is the 14th-floor ***Observation Deck at Independence Wharf***, where you can enjoy a spectacular view of the Boston waterfront without spending a cent. Check in with the security guard at the front desk (you'll need to show an ID) and take the elevators to the top to see the city from high above, including the Fort Point Channel, Boston Harbor,

Foodie Neighborhood: The North End

The first Italian immigrants came to the North End in the late 1800s. With its narrow streets, redbrick tenements, and the smell of garlic in the air, the neighborhood still has a movie-set quality about it. Choosing among the nearly one hundred restaurants packed in the North End can be hard, so here is a list of some of my favorite places.

A classic oyster bar is a fine place for a quick stop at any time of the day or night. Inevitably, there is a line out the door at **Neptune Oyster** (617-742-3474; neptuneoyster .com), located at 63 Salem Street. The mirrored zinc raw bar is a buzzy backdrop to the hum of conversation punctuated by laughter; diners sit elbow to elbow, sipping wine and slurping the briny goodness of freshly shucked oysters. This is where the cool kids hang.

Just down the street, at 93 Salem Street, **Antico Forno** (617-723-6733; anticofornoboston.com) is an absolute staple in the neighborhood for its pizza, top-notch pastas, and simple, honest dishes like braised pork shank with polenta. *Antico forno* means "ancient oven"; the brick wood-fired hearth reaches seven hundred degrees, achieving pizza with a crispy crust that still has a good chew. It also turns out lovely baked pastas; the marvelously cheesy baked rigatoni and sausage is a menu mainstay.

Located at 290 Hanover Street, the first Italian caffe in the neighborhood opened in 1929 and was a natural gathering place for the neighborhood's Italian immigrants. With its cozy bistro tables, marble floors, and a copper-tin ceiling, it is hard not to fall in love with **Caffe Vittoria** (617-227-7606; caffevittoria.com). It's a wonderful spot to take a break and relax with a coffee and cannoli. In the evening, it is a perfect perch for night

and Logan Airport just beyond. Did I mention this is free? Hours are daily from 10 a.m. to 5 p.m.

Art enthusiasts may want to duck into the **_Langham Hotel Boston_** (617-451-1900; langhamhotels.com), which showcases two surprisingly famous (and fabulous) murals. In its former life, the nine-story Beaux Arts–style building was the home of the Boston Federal Reserve. In 1920 the bank commissioned a young artist, Needham-born N. C. Wyeth, to paint two panels honoring historic events that laid the foundations of American finance. Wyeth, principally known as a Scribner's illustrator for children's books like *Treasure Island* and *Robin Hood*, considered the commission an opportunity to prove himself a "serious" painter. One mural depicts George Washington, along with chief Revolutionary War financier Robert Morris and everyone's favorite Founding Father and first secretary of the treasury, Alexander Hamilton. On the opposite wall, Abraham Lincoln confers with his secretary of the treasury, Salmon Chase (instrumental in establishing the IRS and creating the national banking system). Ultimately, acceptance by the art world may have eluded N. C. Wyeth; although the ambition was realized by his son Andrew, owls in search of a nightcap, as it is open until midnight every day and has a full liquor license. Order a caffe coretto, "correct coffee," and your espresso will come with a shot of alcohol.

Located at 257 Hanover Street, *Modern Pastry* (617-523-3783; modernpastry.com) may be borderline touristy, but it is a legendary Italian American bakery that has been around for more than eighty years. Your hunt for the perfect North End cannoli ends here. Modern fills each tender cannoli shell with perfectly balanced (not too sweet) ricotta to order. It's hard to understand why more people don't know that there's also a restaurant under Modern Pastry, but it is a secret that should definitely get out—especially when all the restaurants on Hanover Street are overflowing. Walk down the stairs next door at 263 Hanover Street to *Modern Underground*, a speakeasy-style space where there's usually an Italian soccer match playing silently on the TV above the bar. Take your pick from Italian American dishes such as chicken Parmesan, ravioli with vodka sauce, and Caesar salad. Or channel Frank Sinatra and order a martini. Note: Modern Pastry is cash only, but Modern Underground takes credit cards.

Salumeria Italiana (617-523-8743; salumeriaitaliana.com), at 151 Richmond Street, has been a neighborhood anchor since 1962. Expat Italians and tourists alike are drawn by the shop's high-quality Italian ingredients. Find extra-virgin olive oils, hard-to-find pantry staples like salt-packed anchovies, and aged balsamic vinegar so thick that you can spread it on bread. Those in the know come for made-to-order porchetta or caprese sandwiches to eat at the Greenway picnic tables. Grab a number at the deli counter and brace for a wait, but the people watching is great, and there are always generous samples of salami and cheese to be had.

who became a near-mythic figure of American twentieth-century painting. The Langham Hotel Boston is in the heart of the Financial District, at 250 Franklin Street. The paintings are in the hotel's Wyeth function room on the second floor; just be sure to ask at the front desk if the room is open and available for viewing.

The creeping gentrification of the North End is nothing new, but in certain places the old North End remains. Just off Hanover Street, in the alley between 4 and 8 Battery Street, is a small door with rows of Catholic saint figurines, flowerpots filled with geraniums, and a handmade sign that reads, "Mock all and sundry things, but leave the saints alone." It's not unlike the little wayside shrines you might stumble upon in villages throughout Italy. Behind the door is a room filled with more statues, crosses, and prayer cards. Lifelong North-Ender Peter Baldassari has been collecting saint memorabilia since 1991, and he loves talking to visitors about his hobby, the history of the saints, martyrdom, and miracles. If you want to see inside the shrine and visit with Baldassari, *All Saints Way* is generally open for visitors in the early afternoon on weekdays and from 9:30 a.m. to noon on weekends.

At just ten feet wide, the tiny four-story home at 44 Hull Street in the North End is the narrowest in the city. Located across the street from Copps Burying Ground and sandwiched between two brick townhomes, the **Skinny House** dates from the late 1850s. Urban legend describes the house as a "spite" house, built as the result of a family feud between brothers in the years after the Civil War to block the view. These days, historians believe that the house is probably what has survived of one-half of a narrow, double wood-frame house—so not built out of revenge at all. The two-bedroom, one-bath house is currently a private family home.

With its wide boulevards shaded by magnolia trees and lined with stately brownstones, trendy boutiques, and the city's tallest skyscrapers, Boston's **Back Bay** neighborhood offers a juxtaposition of old-world charm and modern luxury.

Foodie Neighborhood: Chinatown

Boston's Chinatown is in the heart of downtown and was once known as South Cove. Like the Back Bay, it was enlarged by landfill in the 1830s on tidal marsh. By the 1890s, the development of South Station and the creation of garment industry jobs in the area brought the city's first wave of Chinese immigrants. The neighborhood is still a tight-knit Chinese American community; however, lately it is getting younger and more gentrified—and it's booming.

Boston's Chinatown has always been delicious; the city's first Chinese restaurant, Ho Far Low, opened in 1875. Today the neighborhood is an epicurean hot spot packed with dim sum palaces, mom-and-pop restaurants, grocery stores and many, many boba tea shops. It is also intimidating. Even a lot of Bostonians don't know this neighborhood. But Chinatown is totally doable on your own. Whatever you are in the mood for, come hungry as you explore this intriguing neighborhood.

An elaborate **Chinatown Gate** and a pair of imperial white fu lions frame the entrance to Boston's Chinatown at the intersection of Beach Street and Surface Road. This also marks the southernmost point of the **Rose Kennedy Greenway Park** (617-292-0020; rosekennedygreenway.org), which welcomes visitors with traditional Asian design elements, a serpentine walkway, and a public fountain that evokes a shallow stream all landscaped with a mix of plants native to Asia, like gingkoes, rhododendrons, and bamboo.

Behind the black velvet curtain at 9A Tyler Street, **Shojo** (617-482-8887; shojoboston .com) bridges the gap between the old and the new with modern Pan-Asian fusion dishes and inspired craft cocktails. The urban/industrial space features exposed brick and ductwork and an anime graffiti mural against a backdrop of classic kung fu movies that play on repeat over the bar. Nearly everyone orders the duck-fat fries—a version of

Today it is difficult to imagine that this neighborhood was once marshy tideland. Boston lost its hills for what was then a massive public works project; much of the landfill to create the city's westward expansion came from cutting down the three hills of Beacon Hill's Trimount Peak (later becoming "Tremont" and the name of a nearby street). When the landfill project was completed in 1882, it nearly doubled the size of the city.

Secret alleys can lead to the most unexpected travel experiences. Case in point? Walk down Public Alley 437 (at the intersection of Arlington Street and the Newbury Hotel), where a **Puppet Lending Library** (617-262-2031; puppetco-op.org) makes its home in the basement of a church. Ring the bell next to the wooden hobbit-size door to gain entrance to Sara Peattie's atelier—a glorious repository of hundreds of puppet creations, including giant dancing cats, magical sea creatures, and flying dragons. Peattie is a master puppeteer, world renowned for creating the papier-mâché puppets that have become an

chili cheese fries with a meat/bean curd sauce on top. There's also always a variety of stuffed seasonal bao; the Shojo pig bun features smoked barbecue pork and kimchi with barbecue sauce.

The no-frills storefront at 695 Washington Street is a small restaurant with the typically large menu found at older Chinese places, but what keep diners coming back to **Dumpling Café** (617-338-8858; dumplingcafe.com) are the best soup dumplings in town. The juicy dumplings are filled with pork and served in a deep, slurpable broth. To balance things out, order the numbingly spicy sliced fish Sichuan style. Bonus: Most dishes are under $10, which means you can order a lot without spending a ton.

Cozy, comforting hot pot is a platter of vegetables and thinly sliced meat or seafood that you add to your own savory, bubbling broth and then dip in an abundance of sauces—DIY cooking at its very best. **Q Restaurant** (857-350-3968; thequsa.com) at 660 Washington Street is a mainstay of the Boston hot pot scene; they are particularly known for their spicy mala broth and for offering higher-end meat options like Wagyu rib eye. Very good sushi and great cocktails round out the menu; it's no wonder that this is a favorite of the nearby Tufts Medical Center community.

Dim sum stalwart **Hei La Moon** (617-338-8813; heilamoonma.com) has recently moved and is now at 83 Essex Street. It's a bright and modern space, but, yes, they still have the carts stacked with steamer baskets that reveal tender shrimp dumplings, fatty pork riblets, and chicken feet.

C-Market (617-338-8811; cmartboston.com) specializes in Asian ingredients that will take your cooking up a notch. Pick up soy sauce, chili paste, dumpling wrappers, and other pantry essentials as well as hard-to-find ingredients like fermented black bean and Japanese seaweed. It's located at 50 Herald Street and bigger than most in the neighborhood; it's easier to navigate, and high turnover means everything is fresh.

integral part of Boston's First Night parade. Public visiting hours are Tuesday from 2 p.m., by appointment or by chance.

Back Bay office warriors scurry past the Art Deco double bronze doors of 330 Stuart Street, oblivious to the building's history as the corporate headquarters of the Salada Tea Company from 1917 until the early 1950s. The massive twelve-foot-high doors are fanciful in their design and tell the story of tea cultivation in Ceylon (now Sri Lanka). Depicted in high-relief bronze are tea flowers and berries, clipper ships, elephants, and shirtless men wearing loincloths. When installed in 1927, the **Salada Tea Doors** were considered both exotic and scandalous. What's behind these extraordinary doors today? Appropriately, another Boston corporate headquarters—that of Liberty Mutual Insurance.

Boston is rather famous for its tea parties. And **Afternoon Tea at the Boston Public Library** (781-763-1360; librarytea.com) is one of the city's best-kept secrets. The 1895 Renaissance Revival building at 700 Boylston Street was designed by Charles McKim (he later designed New York City's Penn Station) and takes up an entire city block. The Tea Room is a large, sunlit space with floor-to-ceiling windows overlooking the stunning garden of the library's Italianate courtyard. On the three-tier stand are seasonal sandwiches, scones, and decadent pastries, all served on fine china and white linen and with a variety of tea. Indulge in a glass of fizz or tea-infused cocktails. Afternoon tea is offered Wednesday through Sunday, with seatings at 11 a.m., 1 p.m., and 3 p.m. Reservations are essential.

trivia

The weather beacon atop the twenty-six-story Art Deco office tower at 200 Berkeley Street, popularly known as the "Old John Hancock Building," has been a local icon since 1950, predicting the weather and helping residents and visitors to know whether they need an umbrella or heavy coat as they head out the door. Bostonians know they simply need to look up for a quick forecast decoding the signals with a handy rhyming mnemonic: *Steady blue, clear view. Flashing blue, clouds due. Steady red, rain ahead. Flashing red, snow instead* (or, during the baseball season, the Red Sox game has been called because of rain!).

The **Isabella Stewart Gardner Museum** (617-566-4101; gardnermuseum.org) is the kind of place where locals bring out-of-town guests they wish to impress. Established in 1903 and modeled after a Venetian Renaissance palazzo, it's an intimate museum that offers a celebrated collection of old master paintings (including Vermeer and Rembrandt) that reflect the convention-be-damned sensibility of its creator, Boston socialite Isabella Stewart Gardner.

El Jaleo by John Singer Sargent (one of Gardner's artist friends) is a museum highlight—a dark, moody piece depicting a Spanish flamenco dancer accompanied by guitarists. Titian's painting *The Rape of Europa* is also not to be missed; it is considered one of the most important Renaissance paintings in North America.

In 1990 the Gardner Museum was the scene of a sensational art heist of thirteen works worth a collective $500 million. The pieces have yet to be recovered, and empty frames stand in for the stolen paintings.

The museum is beloved for its verdant inner courtyard, blooming with flowers year-round (there is a skylight roof) and is one of the most serene spots in all New England, especially in winter.

Located in Boston's Fenway neighborhood at 25 Evans Way, the museum is open Friday through Monday and Wednesday from 11 a.m. to 4 p.m. and Thursday from 11 a.m. to 8 p.m. Admission is $20 for adults and free for children. The Gardner is closed on Tuesday.

Also, as this part of the city is a restaurant desert, you would do well to have lunch at the museum's Café G, which features classic ladies-who-lunch fare like cold poached salmon salad; Gruyère and mushroom quiche, and a charcuterie plate to be accompanied by rosé sangria (in keeping with the El Jaleo theme).

The city loves its Patriots, Celtics, and Bruins, but Boston is a baseball town. Built in 1912, Fenway Park is home to the Red Sox and the oldest baseball stadium in the majors; it embodies the essence of baseball and nostalgia for a simpler time. Fenway Park is one of the city's top attractions, attracting fans of all persuasions. But you can visit Fenway Park without buying a game ticket or taking the stadium tour. The secret? Beneath Fenway's center field seats, in what used to be the opposing team's batting cages, is **Bleacher Bar** (617-262-2424; bleacherbarboston.com), where you can have a beer and some wings and enjoy the view of the fabled thirty-seven-foot-high Green Monster wall and the Citgo sign in the distance through a bank of floor-to-ceiling windows overlooking the field. When there is a game, giant garage-style doors come down; fans can see out, but the players can't see in. How awesome is that? Bleacher Bar's address is 82A Lansdowne Street; they don't take reservations, so get there well in advance to score a seat for the game. An under-the-radar strategy to beat the crowds is to come three to four hours early on game day and catch batting practice. You're welcome.

For many, the **Boston Symphony Orchestra** (617-266-1200; bso.org) is the city's other hometown team. The BSO was founded in 1881 by businessman and philanthropist Henry Lee Higginson (he was the Jeff Bezos or Elon Musk of his day). Symphony Hall was Higginson's vision too; he funded the building's construction in the newly fashionable Back Bay Fens neighborhood, choosing architect Charles McKim (he had just finished the Boston Public

Library) and a young Harvard physicist, Wallace Sabine, to work out the details of the acoustics. Opened in 1900 to much fanfare, Symphony Hall is acoustically still considered one of the world's top classical music venues. Located at 301 Massachusetts Avenue, the season at Symphony Hall runs September through June. Boston Symphony Orchestra concerts feature dynamic Latvian conductor Andris Nelsons at the helm. Keith Lockhart is the beloved longtime conductor of the Boston Pops, which plays lighter, more contemporary fare during the spring. Lockhart also conducts the Holiday Pops, which take place in December.

The BSO "Behind the Scenes Tour" is one of the rarest regularly scheduled tours offered in the entire city—it is quite special if you can snag it. Tours are offered October through May; usually on Wednesday and Saturday (check online for time). You'll get a peek behind the stage, visit the musicians' locker rooms, and walk through the organized chaos of basement corridors lined with practice rooms and instrument luggage trunks. Tours are free, but you need to register in advance.

Few visitors notice the pretty, perfumed **Kelleher Rose Garden** (617-522-2700; emeraldnecklace.org) tucked away at the nearby Back Bay Fens. The garden was designed by Arthur Shurcliff, a protégé of Frederick Law Olmsted, in the 1920s. It is charmingly formal and old-fashioned. The garden is centered on a fountain, with varieties that pop with color and rambling roses that form scented arbors. The garden showcases 1,500 rose plants and more than 200 mostly modern cultivars, including tea roses, grandifloras, and showy floribundas. Find the entrance to the garden at 73 Park Drive.

For a city with a short growing season, Boston has a surprising number of notable public gardens. A collection of trees from all corners of the world call Harvard University's **Arnold Arboretum** (617-524-1718; arboretum.harvard .edu) home. Established in 1872 in Boston's Jamaica Plain neighborhood at 125 The Arborway, the park was designed by Frederick Law Olmsted as part of the Emerald Necklace, the seven-mile string of public parks that spans the city. For many Bostonians, the park is a perfect place for a stroll and evokes a sense of Victorian style in the twenty-first century. It's no wonder that the Arnold Arboretum was used as a set location for the 2019 movie adaptation of *Little Women*. The Arnold Arboretum represents a unique collaboration; the park is owned by the City of Boston, and the arboretum is managed by Harvard University. Parking is best along the Arborway, and the Hunnewell Building, which houses the visitor center, is just inside the gate. From here it is a short walk to the Explorers Garden, the quarter-mile path highlights some of the arboretum's oldest specimens, including a Franklin tree that astonishingly dates from 1884. While the 281-acre site is renowned for its range of conifers and deciduous trees, the arboretum also features important collections of bonsai, lilacs, and rhododendrons. Don't miss the easy walk to the summit of Bussey Hill, which affords a wonderful view of the Boston skyline in the distance. The park is free and open every day of the year from sunrise to sunset.

The **Museum of Bad Art** (781-44-6757; museumofbadart.org) is, in a word, odd. MOBA's mission is to bring the "worst of art to the widest of audiences." Founded in 1993, its permanent collection numbers some seven hundred pieces of a wide range of inartistic ability (many of which have been found at dumpsters or yard sales), of which thirty are showcased at any one time. The museum has moved locations several times over the years; its current space is located within the **Dorchester Brewing Company** facility at 1250 Massachusetts Avenue and is open during taproom hours Sunday and Monday from 11:30 a.m. to 9 p.m., Tuesday through Thursday from 11:30 a.m. to 10 p.m., and Friday and Saturday from 11:30 a.m. to 11 p.m. Dorchester Brewing Company's craft beer most certainly complements and enhances the art; admission is free.

Smack dab in the middle of a residential street in Boston's Roxbury neighborhood, **Bully Boy Distillers** (617-442-6000; bullyboydistillers.com) is a destination distillery that very much has the feel of being off the beaten track. Brothers Will and Dave Willis began making small-batch rum, whiskey, and vodka in a nearby warehouse in 2011—and haven't looked back since. Bully Boy's sales are booming, and its expanded industrial-chic manufacturing facility at 44 Cedric Street now features both a classic speakeasy saloon-style tasting room and a cocktail garden that in fine weather is a great place to hang out. Enjoy the Bully Boy old-fashioned; it is the best anywhere. Tasting room hours are Thursday and Friday 5 p.m. to 11 p.m., Saturday 1 p.m. to 11 p.m., and Sunday 1 p.m. to 6 p.m. Distillery tours are $10 and offered on Thursday evening and Saturday and Sunday afternoon; check the website for times.

Continuing with the drinking theme, when good weather finally rolls around, the beer garden at **Notch Brewing** (617-548-2947; notchbrewing .com) might just have you believe that you are in Bavaria rather than Brighton (or Brooklyn, as it is very much a neighborhood hipster vibe). There is loads of outdoor seating with mingle-friendly picnic tables where you can sample a solid lineup of Czech- and German-style lagers, some of which are brewed on-site. Notch is located at 525 Western Avenue, which is the old speedway, a harness racing track that was built along the Boston bank of the Charles River in 1899. Notch is a beer hall too, so it is open year-round. It also offers draft and canned beer to go.

Boston restaurant darling Joanne Chang is most known for Flour, her chain of ten wildly popular bakery cafés that dot the city. Lesser known is **Myers &**

Chang at 1145 Washington Street in the South End (617-542-5200; myersand chang.com), which she opened in 2007 with her husband, Christopher Myers. The menu captures the flavors of classic Chinese/Taiwanese cuisine along with dishes that skew elevated street food from Vietnam, Malaysia, and beyond. It's the kind of place where you will order dish after dish, on top of all that you have already irresponsibly ordered. Clever, tropical cocktails add to the bustle. Greatest hits include the sweet potato and Chinese sausage fritters and the wild boar dan dan noodles. If it's on the menu, the fish taco with kimchi salsa, cilantro crema, and pickled red cabbage is a winner.

A museum that focuses on the history of the Boston water supply may sound a bit dull, but the *Metropolitan Waterworks Museum* (617-277-0065; waterworksmuseum.org) is anything but. Located at 2450 Beacon Street, on Boston's border with the city of Newton, the museum is housed in Boston's former water pumping station, a glorious 1888 redbrick and Roxbury puddingstone Romanesque building, constructed during an age when public works buildings were constructed with both functionality and inspiring aesthetics in mind.

Inside, the Great Engines Hall is the museum's centerpiece attraction, housing three massive Industrial Age engines that pumped water to Boston's taps from the late 1800s until the station was decommissioned in the 1970s. Of late, the permanent exhibits on Boston's watery past, including combating the 1849 cholera outbreak and the city's nineteenth-century advances in the battle for public health, have been getting a lot of interest by museumgoers.

The Waterworks Museum is small and doesn't take more than an hour to see, so it is easy to fit into even the busiest itinerary. The museum is open Wednesday through Friday 11 a.m. to 4 p.m., Saturday 10 a.m. to 3 p.m., and Sunday 11 a.m. to 4 p.m. Admission is free.

Cambridge

The Charles River divides Boston from the city of Cambridge. Home to both Harvard and MIT, the city's reputation as "The People's Republic of Cambridge" has more than a little truth to it. Visiting Cambridge is a heady mix of old and new; history and academic tradition, cultural diversity, and youthful activism.

Getting from Boston to Cambridge is easy; taking the T Red Line from downtown's Park Street station to Harvard Square is a straight shot. Driving from Boston to Cambridge takes only minutes as well; there are eight bridges crossing the Charles that connect the two cities, so take your pick.

Go off the beaten path altogether, and admire the cinematic Boston skyline from the water.

Paddle Boston (617-965-5110; paddleboston.com) offers guided ninety-minute small-group kayak tours along the Charles River.

After a quick crash course on how to paddle and steer, off you go, paddling the tea-colored Charles right between Boston and Cambridge, with views of the Massachusetts State House and Back Bay's John Hancock and Prudential skyscrapers as you glide by sailboats and scullers and pass under the redbrick Weeks Footbridge and past the Harvard University campus.

The guides are super at helping even absolute beginners feel confident and safe on the water as they regale the group with stories about Boston history as well as pointing out wildlife. The Paddle Boston Boathouse is under the Cambridge side of the Longfellow Bridge at 15 Broad Canal Way. Tours are offered early May through October; tickets are $59 for adults and $55 for children.

Although located just outside touristy Harvard Square, the *Longfellow House–Washington's Headquarters National Historic Site* (617-876-4491; nps.gov/long) is one of those places that still manages to be undiscovered—except by true history nerds.

The yellow clapboard house at 105 Brattle Street was built in 1759 for wealthy loyalist John Vassall. The street was nicknamed "Tory Road," as several loyalist families lived on this part of Brattle Street at the time of the Revolutionary War. By 1774, the prospect of revolutionary unrest forced the Vassall family to hightail it back to England—never to return.

The grand house was then commandeered by the Continental Army and served as the headquarters of General George Washington during the Siege of Boston from 1775 to 1776. Ultimately, Washington prevailed, and the British were forced to evacuate after the colonists successfully fortified Dorchester Heights with cannons taken from Fort Ticonderoga. It was during these nine months in Cambridge that Washington developed the skills to become the key nationalizing figure of the Revolution.

Sixty years later, the property became the family home of Henry Wadsworth Longfellow. He wrote some of his most famous works here—"Paul Revere's Ride," "The Song of Hiawatha," and "The Courtship of Miles Standish"—epic poems that inspired a young nation.

Behind the house, the formal gardens are open to the public year-round and are considered a hush-hush sanctuary by locals who enjoy reading a good book outdoors. The gardens also host poetry readings and concerts in the summer months.

After all that history, you may be craving a snack. Take a stroll toward Harvard Square stopping at 52 Brattle Street. *L.A. Burdick* (617-491-4340; burdick chocolate.com) is a local institution that feels like the kind of charming and cozy pastry shop you would stumble upon in Paris or Salzburg. It's a favorite of both locals and tourists for coffee and a slice of cake. The Herrentorte, an eleven-layer sponge cake with lemon butter cream and enrobed with dark chocolate, is a marvel. A box of L.A. Burdick's whimsical handmade chocolates (shaped like bees, penguins, and mice) makes a terrific souvenir.

A cemetery may seem an odd destination to tour on vacation; but as a unique urban sanctuary connected with nature, history, and art, it is hard to stay away. Established in 1831 as a solution to Boston's rising population and overcrowding of church burial grounds, **Mount Auburn Cemetery** (617-547-7105; mountauburn.org) was greatly inspired by the garden cemetery style of Paris's Père Lachaise. The 175-acre grounds are beautifully maintained with wide walkways, manicured meadows, hidden corners, and secret paths. Mount Auburn is a National Historic Landmark and an arboretum that attracts more than 200,000 visitors a year. Mount Auburn has robust public programming that includes guided nature tours and birding walks throughout the year. It's located just outside of Harvard Square at 580 Mount Auburn Street. A map for self-guided tours is available for $1 at the visitor center, which is located just inside the gate. The cemetery is the final resting place of many Boston notables, including colonial-era architect Charles Bulfinch, Gilded Age socialite Isabella Stewart Gardner, and painter Winslow Homer. Poet Henry Wadsworth Longfellow's grave is one of the easiest to find: From the front entrance, walk along Fountain Avenue to the intersection of Catalpa Path. Another popular stop? Climbing the ninety-seven steps of Washington Tower for a panoramic view of the Boston skyline. Note: Mount Auburn Cemetery is an active burial ground, so be respectful of mourners.

Would you be surprised to know that one of Boston's best restaurants is across the street from Mount Auburn? Located on the Cambridge-Watertown line at 1 Belmont Street, **Sofra** (617-661-3161; sofrabakery.com) means "spread" in Turkish, as in the food you would offer the guests at your table at home. Chef-owner Ana Sortun and head pastry chef Maura Fitzpatrick have created a menu of dishes that are full of color and spice, featuring the food of Turkey along with some forays into Lebanese, Greek, and Iranian cuisine. What's on the pastry counter changes daily but will usually include perfectly laminated kouign-aman and orange-scented cardamom morning buns. The lunch menu runs from a chicken and couscous salad with farm greens to a sausage flatbread with pickled peppers and feta. The must-order? The mezze platter featuring beet tzatziki, whipped feta, and hummus topped with pomegranate. The space is tight, and it's super busy on weekends; best to come in the late afternoon on a weekday.

It's a short fifteen-minute drive or ten-minute T ride from Cambridge to the city of Medford. Originally part of Charlestown, today Medford is mostly known as the home of Tufts University. Just a few minutes from campus, the three-story Georgian house that sits at 15 George Street in Medford Square is no ordinary home. It was built in 1733 for Isaac Royall, a loyalist merchant who made his fortune in Antiguan sugarcane and the slave trade. For more than a century, the focus of the **Royall House & Slave Quarters** (781-396-9032; royallhouse.org) was on the "big house." It was considered a charming but obscure New England house museum of elegantly proportioned rooms filled with fine period furniture and china. It was a home fit for royalty—or, rather, faux Royalls. Today, visitors to the estate hear a more balanced history. The estate's cramped slave quarters are the only still-standing slave house in New England. It has been restored to tell the largely untold story of slavery in Massachusetts and, more specifically, of the sixty enslaved people who made the Royalls' lifestyle possible. The house is open June through October on Saturday and Sunday, with tours at 1, 2, and 3 p.m. Admission is $10 for adults and free for children age twelve and under.

Brookline

Brookline was part of Boston until it was incorporated as a separate town in 1705. Brookline is well connected to Boston—it's literally surrounded on all sides by the city, and it's easy enough to take the MBTA or even walk to Boston from either of the town's happening commercial districts: Coolidge Corner and Brookline Village.

The **John F. Kennedy National Historic Site** (617-566-7937; nps.gov/ jofi) is the birthplace and boyhood home of John Fitzgerald Kennedy, America's 35th president and Boston's beloved native son.

The modest two-and-a-half-story house, located at 83 Beals Street in a quiet, leafy neighborhood, offers insight into the world of young "Jack" Kennedy. He was the second of nine children born to Rose and Joseph Kennedy and was delivered here, in his parents' bedroom, on May 29, 1917. JFK lived in this house for only three years; the rapidly expanding Kennedy family outgrew the house and moved to nearby Abbotsford Road in 1920.

After JFK's tragically short presidency, Rose Kennedy bought back her family's former home with the intention of creating a legacy to her son's life. She refurnished the house as it was at JFK's birth; much of the dining room furniture belonged to the Kennedy family, as did the grand piano in the living room. Family mementos include Rose's handwritten notes of her children's developmental milestones, the family christening gown, and Jack's favorite nursery books.

Off the Beaten Path: Kid's Edition

Think of the Franklin Park Zoo and Harvard Museum of Natural History as a locals' secret, overlooked by tourists and overshadowed by Boston's "Big-3" children's attractions: the New England Aquarium, the Museum of Science, and the Children's Museum. Both Franklin Park and the Harvard Museum of Natural History are particularly good places to visit with the stroller set; neither is huge, so they are not overwhelming for little ones.

Set in the heart of Boston's Dorchester neighborhood, the **Franklin Park Zoo** (617-541-5466; zoonewengland.org) was established in 1912. Typical for zoological parks of that time, it began as an ad hoc menagerie of caged exotic animals for public entertainment. Over the years, Franklin Park has evolved to become a recognized leader in animal conservation, managing the breeding of such endangered species as the whooping crane and red river hog. Its education initiatives are noteworthy too, such as providing vet rotations for Harvard medical students. Recently there has been an emphasis on sustainable, high-quality exhibits like Gorilla Grove, which opened in 2022, offering a naturalistic outdoor habitat for the zoo's troop of apes. Other highlights are Franklin Farm to pet the goats and sheep and Kalahari Kingdom to visit the lions where twin brothers Dinari and Kamaia are crowd favorites. The zoo is part of Franklin Park, the city's largest, at 1 Franklin Park Road. Open daily 9 a.m. to 5 p.m. (winter, 9 a.m. to 4 p.m.). Admission is $22.95 for adults, $15.95 for children.

Ice cream is just about everyone's favorite treat after a trip to the zoo. The old fire station at 659 Centre Street houses the headquarters and production facility of **J.P. Licks** (617-524-6740; jplicks.com)—as in Jamaica Plain—Boston's beloved home-grown premium ice cream brand. With a rotating library of more than forty flavors of deliciousness, including brownie batter and maple butter walnut, it can be hard to choose. But you know what to do.

Across the Charles River, in Cambridge, is the **Harvard Museum of Natural History** (617-495-3045; hmnh.harvard.edu). It is the public face of the university—a repository of all aspects of the natural world, from the Great Mammal Hall with its vast collection of taxidermy (many from Harvard-funded research expeditions across the globe in the late nineteenth century) to the Earth and Planetary Gallery, featuring a dazzling 1,600-pound amethyst geode. Kids invariably head straight to Romer Hall and the dinosaurs, which have delighted and educated generations of New England families. Not to be missed are the "Glass Flowers." Commissioned by Harvard in 1891 for the purpose of teaching botany, the astonishingly detailed glass botanical models were crafted by Leopold Blaschka and his son Rudolf over a span of fifty years. The museum is located on the edge of the Harvard University campus at 26 Oxford Street and is open daily from 9 a.m. to 5 p.m. Admission is $15 for adults and $10 for children. If you need a break for lunch, Harvard Square beckons.

Managed by the National Park Service, the house is open for free guided tours from May through October; check the website for times. Tours typically start on the front porch, with rangers showing enlarged photos that capture the charisma of the Kennedy clan, and visitors of a certain age are encouraged to reminisce about where they were on November 22, 1963, when JFK was assassinated.

The National Park Service also runs the ***Frederick Law Olmsted National Historic Site*** (617-566-1689; nps.ov.frla). Frederick Law Olmsted, the architect of Boston's Emerald Necklace and New York City's Central Park, is considered the founder of American landscape design. His two-acre country estate, Fairsted, was both his family home and the headquarters for his landscape architecture firm. Fairsted is a real treat for gardeners. The park service offers guided tours of Olmsted's home and office and a separate guided stroll of the grounds—take both. Fairsted is set away from Brookline Village, among the rolling hills of South Brookline, at 90 Warren Street. The home is open April through December; check the website for days and times. The grounds are open daily from dawn to dusk. Admission is free.

A true hole-in-the-wall, ***Rami's*** (617-738-3577; ramisboston.com) is a much loved traditional falafel spot; it's at 324 Harvard Street (conveniently just a few doors down from the Coolidge Corner Cinema), but if you walk too fast, you might miss it. These are well-constructed sandwiches—pitas that are over-stuffed with fried chickpea balls, Israeli pickles, and cabbage, then slathered with tahini and a house-made hot sauce. Note: Rami's is kosher and closes on Friday at 2 p.m. and is closed all day Saturday.

Lexington

The neighboring towns of Lexington and Concord are inextricably linked by the dramatic story of how area farmers and townspeople took up arms against the British in these woods and fields in the early-morning hours of April 19, 1775. It was the first military battle of the Revolutionary War. The ***Battle Road Trail*** (781-674-1920; nps.gov/mima) connects thirteen historic sites, including the first skirmish on Lexington Common, the Paul Revere Capture site, the standoff at North Bridge, and the ill-fated British column's retreat to Boston.

It's not hard to imagine colonists taking potshots at the British from behind these trees and stone walls. For visitors, it is most definitely the path less traveled, if only because it is nearly five miles long.

The Battle Road Trail is wide and mostly paved (it's also shared with bikers) and well signed along the way. Note that it's a point-to-point walk; the parking lot for the Lexington trailhead is at Fiske Hill (Massachusetts Avenue and Wood Street); the parking lot in Concord is at Meriam's Corner (at Lexington Road). You can start and finish anywhere along this very special trek back in time.

If you are a history buff, you may as well stay at a historic hotel. Just a short walk from Lexington Battle Green, at 2027 Massachusetts Avenue, the design-forward *Inn at Hastings Park* (781-301-6660; innathastingspark .com) is spread over three antique buildings: the 1888 Main House, the 1841 Isaac Mulliken House, and the next-door barn. No expense has been spared to make the twenty-two rooms supremely comfortable yet entirely unique in design; think custom pillow-topped mattresses and luxury linens, marble bathrooms, and bespoke furnishings in classic patterns with punches of bright color as well as the essential navy and white. The library/lounge has an Ivy League design aesthetic and perfectly curated vignettes of books, flowers, and art. The inn's *Town Meeting Bistro* really is the center of town life and is both a hangout and hideaway for area locals. The menu leans modern seasonal American; lunch choices are homey, including clam chowder, a daily quiche and side salad, and a very good burger. In the evening the kitchen turns out more substantial, craveable dishes like honey-brushed duck and spring vegetables and pan-roasted salmon with farro and a pomegranate glaze.

Concord

Like its counterpart Lexington, Concord is home to several Revolutionary War sites, including a part of Minute Man National Historic Park. But in addition to American history, Concord is the cultural cradle of Transcendentalism, the literary and philosophical movement that nurtured some of the country's most formative thinkers and writers of the early nineteenth century.

To tour all the literary destinations in Concord can take two days; visiting *Sleepy Hollow Cemetery* (978-318-3233; concordma.gov) may be a quirky itinerary choice, but it's a really good way to pay tribute to Concord's most famous residents all at once.

This rural garden cemetery is the final resting place of Ralph Waldo Emerson, Henry David Thoreau, Nathaniel Hawthorne, and Louisa May Alcott. These four greats of American literature were also friends and colleagues in life and now are neighbors to one another along Authors Ridge, a gentle hillside under a canopy of trees. A steady stream of fans come to commune with nature, leaving tokens of pine cones, small stones, and posies. Interestingly, Thoreau's grave is always strewn with pencils (his family owned a pencil factory, where he worked for most of adult his life). Alcott's grave stands out too; it is marked with an American flag and a sign that honors her service as a nurse in the Civil War. Sleepy Hollow is an active public cemetery and is located on the outskirts of town at the intersection of Court Lane and Bedford Street. There is good signage to Authors Ridge; hours are daily from 7 a.m. to dusk.

Henry David Thoreau was all about off the beaten path: "I went to the woods because I wanted to live deliberately" wrote Thoreau of his experience living for nearly two years in a tiny hut on the edge of Concord's **Walden Pond** (978-369-3252; mass.gov/locations/walden-pond-state-reservation). His book *Walden* has become part of the American literary canon; its themes of nature and simple living are as relevant today as they were when the book was published in 1854. The pond is now part of Walden Pond State Park. Thoreau's beloved Walden now has a lifeguarded swimming beach, which is mobbed in high summer with families. However, during the rest of the year, it's generally a peaceful 1.7-mile looping amble around the pond's perimeter and through deep forest—still a very Thoreauvian experience. Walden Pond is just off State Route 126; the parking lot is at 915 Walden Street. Parking fees are $8 per car for Massachusetts residents, $30 for nonresidents. At the corner of the parking lot is a replica of Thoreau's cabin—at just ten feet wide and fifteen feet long, it's true tiny house living!

Park picnic perfection can be found two miles up the road at **Nashoba Brook Bakery** (978-318-1999; slowrise.com). Nashoba Brook Bakery specializes in slow-rise breads with stone-ground flours. The tarragon chicken salad on seven-grain bread is a simple pleasure, or order a big, beautiful Reuben on sourdough rye. Besides killer sandwiches, they do excellent ice coffee. Afternoon pick-me-up achieved. The bakery and café share space at 152 Commonwealth Avenue, with both indoor and outdoor seating to enjoy lunch with a view of oak-pine forest and wetlands.

Lincoln

In any season, a drive along Lincoln's winding country back roads is stunning, passing farms, orchards, placid ponds, and swaths of maple trees.

There are few more scenic spots in all Massachusetts than the **DeCordova Sculpture Park & Museum** (781-259-8355; decordova.org). The DeCordova's thirty acres of lawns, field, and forest along the shore of Lincoln's Flint's Pond are populated with some sixty whimsical, often thought-provoking sculptures, most of which were produced by artists working today. *Two Black Hearts*

(1985), an installation of mega-scaled 3,200-pound bronzes by pop artist Jim Dine, is a favorite for many.

The sculpture park is a wonderful place to engage with both nature and contemporary art, while the museum's airy inside galleries feature rotating modern art exhibits. There is also the excellent Twisted Tree Café for coffee drinks and pastries at breakfast and salads, sandwiches, and other light fare for lunch (the soups are stellar).

The museum is located at 51 Sandy Pond Road. In summer it is open daily from 10 a.m. to 5 p.m.; in winter it's open Wednesday through Sunday 10 a.m. to 5 p.m. Admission is $18 for adults, free for children.

Just a mile down the road from Walden Pond, a small, thoroughly modern white house on the crest of a hill stands out in country-posh Lincoln. The house was designed in 1938 by Walter Gropius, father of the Bauhaus design movement, as his family home after moving from Germany to teach at Harvard. The house was integrated with nature; the view from the glass curtain walls was considered of paramount importance; the house's simple shape was conducive to an open floor plan, novel for the time. It was very much a Bauhaus dream house, and the Gropius family lived here until 1969. A modern house museum, **Gropius House** (781-259-8098; historicnewengland.org) is a fine example not only of Gropius's work but also that of his protégé Marcel Breuer. Breuer also lived in Lincoln for a time, and many of the Gropius family's furniture pieces are Breuer prototypes. Breuer's iconic tubular steel chair can be seen in the dining room.

The house address is 68 Baker Bridge Road. Visiting the home is by guided tour only; tours are given Thursday through Sunday on the hour from 11 a.m. to 3 p.m.; admission is $25.

Drumlin Farm (781-259-2200; massaudubon.org) is the headquarters of the Massachusetts Audubon Society. It is a working farm as well as a wildlife sanctuary, and while it doesn't draw big crowds, it offers lots of hikes and other activities that are sure to satisfy outdoor enthusiasts. Four miles of walking trails crisscross the property. Several are easy walking trails, suitable for walkers of all abilities. The half-mile Farm Yard loop brings visitors by the vegetable garden, greenhouse, and barn and is particularly popular with families with children. The Drumlin Trail is also short, but it packs a punch with some uphill sections and the reward of a lovely view of Mount Wachusett in the distance from the top of the drumlin. And as you would expect, conditions here are optimal for birding, so don't forget to bring your binoculars. Drumlin Farm is at 208 South Great Road. Hours are Tuesday through Sunday from 9 a.m. to 5 p.m.; closed on Monday (except holiday Mondays). Admission is $9 for adults and $6 for children.

Afterward, a trip to **Dairy Joy** (508-424-0079) is in order. This roadside ice cream stand is located three miles down State Route 117, at 331 North Avenue, in the town of Weston. Open since 1961, it is a community fixture in these parts for hot dogs, burgers, fried clams, and especially soft-serve ice cream. The signature flavor is Javaberry, a swirled mixture of coffee and raspberry ice cream. Tip: it can be dipped in chocolate to make it even better. Dairy Joy is open seasonally from mid-March through early November; daily from 11:30 a.m. to 6 p.m. Note: It's cash only.

Stamps and letters, boring? Not! Located in the town of Weston, The **Spellman Museum of Postal History** (781-768-8367; spellmanmuseum .org), on the campus of Regis College at 241 Wellesley Street, is a fascinating little museum that explores all things philatelic. Find displays about the 1673 establishment of the nation's first mail service between Boston and New York City along the Boston Post Road, touching letters from Civil War soldiers, and a 1930s-era dress fashioned from more than two thousand stamps. You can pull out the drawers to discover colorful worldwide postage gems or start your own collection, choosing from among the thousands of stamps in the terrific gift shop. Hours are noon to 5 p.m. Thursday through Sunday (closed summer Sundays). Admission is $8 for adults and $3 for children.

Places to Stay in Greater Boston

BOSTON

AC Hotel by Marriott at Cleveland Circle
395 Chestnut Hill Ave.
(617) 730-3660
marriott.com

Boston Park Plaza
50 Park Plaza at Arlington St.
(617) 426-2000
bostonparkplaza.com

College Club of Boston
44 Commonwealth Ave.
(617) 536-9510
thecollegeclubofboston
.com

Eliot Hotel
370 Commonwealth Ave.
(617) 267-1607
eliothotel.com

Godfrey Hotel Boston
505 Washington St.
(617) 804-2000
godfreyhotelboston.com

Inn @ St. Botolph
99 Saint Botolph St.
(617) 236-8099
innatstbotolph.com

Newbury Guest House
261 Newbury St.
(617) 670-6000
newburyguesthouse.com

The Verb Hotel
1271 Boylston St.
(617) 566-4500
theverbhotel.com

CAMBRIDGE

Freepoint Hotel Cambridge
220 Alewife Brook Pkwy.
(617) 491-8000
freepointhotel.com

Hotel 1868
1868 Massachusetts Ave.
(617) 499-2998
hotel1868.com

Porter Square Hotel
1924 Massachusetts Ave.
(617) 499-3399
theportersquarehotel.com

LEXINGTON

Inn at Hastings Park
2027 Lexington Ave.
(781) 301-6660
innathastingspark.com

CONCORD

Concord's Colonial Inn
48 Monument Sq.
(978) 369-9200
concordscolonialinn.com

North Bridge Inn
21 Monument St.
(978) 371-0014
northbridgeinn.com

Places to Eat in Greater Boston

BOSTON

Beehive
541 Tremont St.
(617) 423-0069
beehiveboston.com
Global cuisine and live jazz

Brassica Kitchen+Café
3710 Washington St.
(617) 477-4569
brassicakitchen.com
Farm-to-table

Brewer's Fork
7 Moulton St.
(617) 337-5703
brewersfork.com
Gastropub

Café Landwer
651 Boylston St.
(857) 250-2902
landwercafe.com
Israeli

Chickadee
21 Drydock Ave.
(617) 531-5591
chickadeerestaurant.com
Mediterranean

Deuxave
371 Commonwealth Ave.
(617) 517-5915
deuxave.com
French

El Pelon Taqueria
92 Peterborough St.
(617) 262-9090
elpelon.com
Mexican

Eventide
1321 Boylston St.
(617) 545-1060
eventideoysterco.com
Seafood

The Fed at the Langham
250 Franklin St.
(617) 956-8765
langhamhotels.com
Cocktail bar

Grill 23 & Bar
161 Berkeley St.
(617) 542-2255
grill23.com
Steak

The Haven
284 Armory St.
(617) 524-2836
thehavenjp.com
Scottish

Legal Seafoods
270 Northern Ave.
(617) 477-2900
legalseafoods.com
Seafood

Mida
782 Tremont St.
(617) 936-3490
midarestaurant.com
Italian

Paramount
44 Charles St.
(617) 720-1152
Paramountboston.com
Breakfast/diner

Parish Café & Bar
361 Boylston St.
(617) 2427-4777
parishcafe.com
Sandwiches

Picco
513 Tremont St.
(617) 927-0066
piccoboston.com
Pizza and ice cream

Pier 6 Charlestown
1 Eighth St.
(617) 337-0054
pier6boston.com
Seafood

Row 34
383 Congress St.
(617) 553-5900
row34.com
Seafood

Sportello
348 Congress St.
(617) 737-1234
sportelloboston.com
Italian

Sweet Cheeks Q
1381 Boylston St.
(617) 266-1300
sweetcheeksq.com
Barbecue

TOP ANNUAL EVENTS

JANUARY

First Night
Boston
firstnightboston.org

APRIL

Boston Marathon
Boston
baa.org

Patriots Day Reenactments
Lexington/Lincoln/Concord

MAY

Franklin Park Kite & Bike Festival
Boston
(617) 442-4141
franklinparkcoalition.org

Lilac Sunday
Boston
(617) 524-1718
arboretum.harvard.edu

JUNE

Boston Hong Kong Dragon Boat Festival
Boston/Cambridge
(617) 371-7890
bostondragonboat.org

Cambridge Arts River Festival
Cambridge
(617) 349-4380
cambridgema.gov

Donna Summer Disco Party
Boston
(617) 635-3911
boston.gov

JULY

Harborfest
Boston
(617) 439-7700
bostonharborfest.com

AUGUST

North End Italian Feasts & Processions
Boston
northendboston.com

SEPTEMBER

What the Fluff? Festival
Sommerville
(617) 955-0080
flufffestival.com

OCTOBER

Head of the Charles Regatta
Boston/Cambridge
(617) 868-6200
hocr.org

Toro
1704 Washington St.
(617) 536-4300
toro-restaurant.com
Spanish tapas

Troquet
107 South St.
(617) 695-9463
troquetboston.com
French/wine bar

Uni
370-A Commonwealth Ave.
(617) 536-7200
uni-boston.com
Japanese

BROOKLINE

Barcelona Wine Bar
1700 Beacon St.
(617) 264-8900
barcelonawinebar.com
Spanish

Refueling

If you are on the go in Boston, it's good to have a handy list of reliable local spots for a quick bite. These citywide chains mean that tasty delights are always within reach so you can get on with your day and see what you came to see.

Anna's Taqueria (annastaqueria.com). This chain of fast-casual eateries boasts five outposts in Boston and Cambridge and is celebrated among college students and the office lunch crowd for its solid menu of traditional, affordable burritos and tacos with heaping portions of rice and beans on the side.

Clover Food Lab (cloverfoodlab.com). This chain of bright, minimalist vegetarian cafés started out in 2008 as a food truck parked at MIT and has over the years morphed into a dozen brick-and-mortar restaurants. The menu changes with the seasons. There's a brussels sprout sandwich and an Impossible Meatball sub, but Clover Food Lab customers are a cultish bunch, and the chickpea fritter sandwich (a pita filled with fried chickpea balls, hummus, and pickled vegetables, drizzled with tahini) and the rosemary french fries are always there for them.

Dunkin' (dunkindonuts.com). The first Dunkin' Donuts shop opened in Quincy in 1950, and today the company's world headquarters is in Canton. Bay Staters really do "run on Dunkin'"—there are 60 Dunks in Boston and more than 1,100 in Massachusetts. Walk up to the counter, order a "regular" (coffee with cream and sugar), and you are one of us.

Flour (flourbakery.com). Bostonians can't get enough of Joanne Chang's stylish and inviting bakery cafés—there are now nine spread across the city. For breakfast, come early for coffee, iced lattes, and the award-winning sticky buns—they often sell out. For lunch, it must be the smoked bacon with arugula and sundried tomato—it's one very fancy BLT.

Tasty Burger (tastyburger.com). Sometimes nothing but a burger will do. Tasty burgers are straightforward and budget friendly, and they always hit the spot. Regulars tend to order the Big Tasty—a one-third-pound beef patty served on a buttered, toasted potato bun; stacked with lettuce, tomatoes, pickles, and onions, topped with American cheese; and slathered with special sauce. Tasty has one location in Harvard Square and four in Boston; the restaurants all have a fun burger joint vibe with a bonus—they serve beer and wine too.

Tatte (tatte.com). Tatte, Yiddish for "daddy," is a local chain of artisan bakery cafés with twenty outposts in the metropolitan Boston area—and still growing. Inside, the vibe is simple: airy and white, with bistro seating and long communal wood tables. It's a laid-back crowd who enjoy an all-day menu influenced by Mediterranean and Israeli traditions. Among the top choices are the cinnamon rolls with buttermilk icing, the prosciutto, the pea tartine with a poached egg, and the short-rib grilled cheese sandwiches.

Cutty's
284 Washington St.
(617) 505-1844
cuttyfoods.com
Deli

Fugakyu
1280 Beacon St.
(617) 734-1268
fugakyu.net
Japanese

Publick House
1648 Beacon St.
(617) 277-2880
publickhousebrookline.com
Gastropub

CAMBRIDGE

Area Four
500 Technology Sq.
(617) 758-4444
areafour.com
Pizza

Alden & Harlow
40 Brattle St.
(617) 864-2100
aldenharlow.com
American

Café Sushi
1105 Massachusetts Ave.
(617) 492-0434
cafesushicambridge.com
Sushi

Giula
1682 Massachusetts Ave.
(617) 441-2800
giularestaurant.com
Italian

Harvest
44 Brattle St.
(617) 868-2255
harvestcambridge.com
New England

OTHER ATTRACTIONS

Boston Children's Museum
308 Congress St.
Boston
(617) 426-6500
bostonchildrensmuseum.org

Boston Swan Boats
Boston Public Garden
4 Charles St.
Boston
(617) 522-1966
swanboats.com

Concord Museum
53 Cambridge Turnpike
Concord
(978) 369-9763
concordmuseum.org

Fenway Park
4 Jersey St.
Boston
(617) 226-6666
mlb.com/redsox

Harvard Art Museums
32 Quincy St.
Cambridge
(617) 495-9400
harvardartmuseums.org

Institute of Contemporary Arts
25 Harbor Shore Dr.
Boston
(617) 478-3100
icaboston.org

Museum of Fine Arts
465 Huntington Ave.
Boston
(617) 267-9300
mfa.org

Museum of Science
1 Science Park
Boston
(617) 723-2500
mos.org

New England Aquarium
1 Central Wharf
Boston
(617) 973-5200
neaq.org

SELECTED CHAMBER OF COMMERCE & TOURISM BUREAUS

Meet Boston
Boston Common
139 Tremont St.
Boston 02111
(888) 733-2678
bostonusa.com

Cambridge Office for Tourism
1374 Massachusetts Ave.
Cambridge 02138
(617) 441-2884
cambridgeusa.org

Greater Merrimack Valley Convention & Visitors Bureau
97 University Ave.
Lowell 01854
(978) 459-6150
merrimackvalley.org

Russell House Tavern
14 JFK St.
(617) 500-3055
russellhousecambridge
.com
Gastropub

The Smoke Shop
8 Holyoke St.
(617) 547-7427
thesmokeshopbbq.com
Barbecue

CONCORD

80 Thoreau
80 Thoreau St.
(978) 318-0008
80thoreau.com
New American

Bedford Farms
60 Thoreau St.
(978) 341-0000
bedfordfarmsicecream.com
Ice cream

Woods Hill Table
24 Commonwealth Ave.
(978) 254-1435
woodshilltable.com
Farm-to-table

LEXINGTON

Il Casale
1727 Massachusetts Ave.
(781) 538-5846
ilcasalelexington.com
Italian

Ma France
46 Massachusetts Ave.
(781) 862-1047
mafrancegourmet.com
French bakery café

Rancatore's
1752 Massachusetts Ave.
(781) 862-5090
rancs.com
Ice cream

SOMERVILLE

Thirsty Scholar
70 Beacon St.
(617) 497-2294
thristyscholarpub.com
Irish

Sarma
249 Pearl St.
(617) 764-4464
sarmarestaurant.com
Mediterranean/Middle
Eastern

North of Boston

Along Massachusetts's Atlantic coast, the North Shore includes the little beach towns just outside the city, like Revere, as well as the legendary seaports of Salem, Gloucester, and Newburyport that extend up to the New Hampshire border. It's an area with an amazing diversity of landscapes: rocky shoreline, sandy beaches, quaint harbor towns, verdant woods, breezy salt marshes—and always and everywhere, legendary fried clams.

The region is dominated by Cape Ann, a peninsula that juts out into the Atlantic and forms the northern edge of Massachusetts Bay. Cape Ann is often referred to as "the other Cape" (as opposed to Cape Cod). It includes the towns of Gloucester, Rockport, Manchester-by-the-Sea, and Essex and has a rugged beauty that is more similar to Maine.

In 1604 French explorer Samuel de Champlain sailed from eastern Canada to the northern New England coast and came ashore around present-day Gloucester Harbor, encountering people of the Pawtucket tribe. In 1623 the first English settlers arrived from Plymouth Colony, establishing a small fishing outpost. The fishing station failed after a few seasons, but some of the survivors moved on, following the Bass River south and founding the village of Salem.

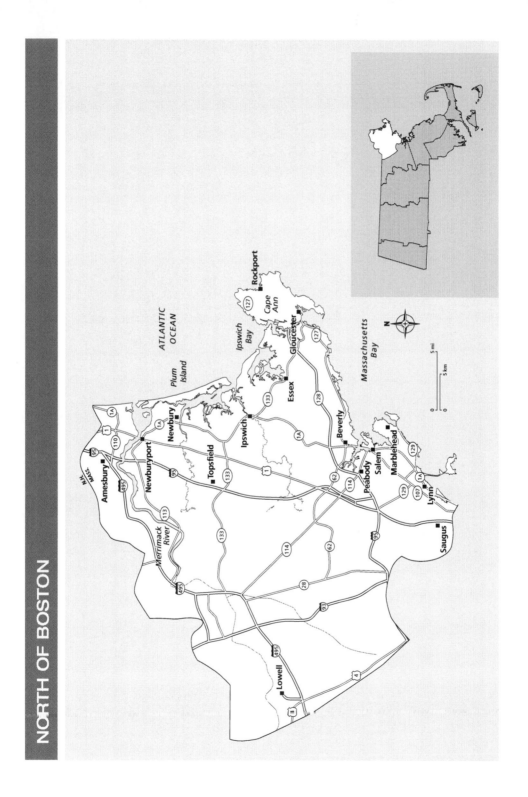

Inland, river-powered mills in Saugus during the mid-1600s and Lowell in the mid-1800s played important roles in the early industrialization of America. The Saugus Iron Works National Historic Site and the Lowell National Historical Park examine the effects of technology and labor in early New England. Both pioneering mill towns are well worth a visit.

Head north out of the city along busy Route 1. Stretching from Maine to Florida, it is one of the country's first interstate highways. The bit that runs from Boston through Saugus captures the kitschy splendor of mid-century Americana with a wonderful collection of roadside landmarks, including a fifty-foot orange dinosaur and a giant cactus sign advertising the dearly departed Hilltop Steakhouse.

AUTHOR'S TOP TEN PICKS

Appleton Farms
219 County Rd.
Ipswich
(978) 356-5728
thetrustees.org

Cape Ann Museum
27 Pleasant St.
Gloucester
(978) 283-0455
capeannmuseum.org

Crane Outdoors
290 Argilla Rd.
Ipswich
(978) 356-3066
thetrustees.org

Halibut Point State Park
4 Gott Ave.
Rockport
(978) 546-2997
mass.gov/locations/
halibut-point-state-park

Lowell National Historical Park
246 Market St.
Lowell
(978) 970-5000
nps.gov/lowe

Lowell's Boat Shop
459 Main St.
Amesbury
(978) 834-0050
lowellsboatshop.com

Parker River National Wildlife Refuge
6 Plum Island Turnpike
Newburyport
(978) 465-5753
fws.gov/refuge/parker-river

Punto Urban Art Museum
91-1 Peabody St.
Salem
(978) 745-8071
puntourbanartmuseum.org

Salem Witch Trials Memorial
24 Liberty St.
Salem
(978) 740-1250
voicesagainstinjustice.org

Saugus Iron Works
244 Central St.
Saugus
(978) 740-1650
nps.gov/sair

The importance of the ***Saugus Iron Works*** (978-740-1650; nps.gov/sair) in shaping early American industry cannot be overestimated. Originally named Hammersmith, the foundry can trace its roots to the 1640s. At the time, iron was necessary for many finished goods: nails for houses and boats, wagon wheels, plows, and kettles. It was worth more than gold and could only be imported from England. Massachusetts Bay Governor John Winthrop saw the need for the fledgling colony to be self-sufficient. Hammersmith was established on the banks of the Saugus River, which provided water for the sophisticated system of hydraulics that drove the wheels to run the machinery. The manufacturing success enriched the colony, helping it become independent from England and laying the foundation of America's iron and steel industry. The twelve-acre industrial site, a historically accurate re-creation of the Puritan-era operation, features a forge, paddlewheels, a rolling mill, a warehouse, and a blacksmith shop. There is also a short nature trail through the very same forest that once fed the blast furnace's insatiable need for fire. Saugus Iron Works is located at

TOP ANNUAL EVENTS

JUNE

St. Peter's Fiesta
Gloucester
stpetersfiesta.org

JULY

Lowell Folk Festival
Lowell
(978) 275-1764
lowellfolkfestival.org

Revere Beach International Sand Sculpting Festival
Revere
reverebeach.com

AUGUST

Salem Heritage Days
Salem
(800) 326-0151
salem.org

Newburyport Yankee Homecoming
Newburyport
yankeehomecoming.com

SEPTEMBER

Gloucester Schooner Festival
Gloucester Harbor
(978) 281-0470
maritimegloucester.org

Trails & Sails
Essex National Heritage Area
(978) 740-0444
trailsandsails.org

OCTOBER

Essex Clam Fest
Essex
(978) 283-1601
capeannchamber.com

Haunted Happenings
Salem
hauntedhappenings.org

244 Central Street and is open from June through October, daily from 10 a.m. to 4 p.m.; admission is free.

Salem

Just fifteen miles northeast of Boston, Salem is infamous for its witchcraft trials of 1692. But there is much more to Salem than witches. For colonial and maritime history, art, architecture, and eccentricity, Salem is a one-of-a-kind city that enchants.

Salem was one of America's first English settlements (established in 1626, it predates Boston), becoming a bustling colonial seaport during the seventeenth and eighteenth centuries. Today, strolling the McIntire Historic District to see the dozens of lovingly maintained mansions of Salem's ruling merchant class is a bona fide attraction. History and art lovers will find much to explore at the Salem Maritime National Historic Site and at the world-class *Peabody Essex Museum*.

During October, Salem becomes the Halloween capital of the world, beginning with the Grand Parade on the first Thursday of the month and culminating with the Witches' Halloween Ball. For more than three centuries, Salem has grappled with the grim past of its witch trials, but these days the city fully embraces modern-day witchy–New Age spiritualism.

A five-minute walk from the Essex Pedestrian Mall is the Point neighborhood. In the early nineteenth century, it was home to French-Canadian immigrants; today Il Punto is largely Latino. Founded in 2017, the *Punto Urban Art Museum* (978-745-8071; puntourbanartmuseum.org) has become Salem's most Instagrammable place. In the span of three blocks there are more than eighty large-scale murals by some of the world's most renowned street artists, including Ruben Ubiera, Chor Boogie, and LeDania. Most of the murals are painted on the sides of the neighborhood's multifamily four-story brick buildings located along Peabody and Lafayette Streets. This outdoor "gallery" explores

City Experiences

City Experiences (617-227-4321; cityexperiences.com) offers daily high-speed ferry service between Boston and Salem. The forty-five-minute ride departs from Boston's Long Wharf, arriving at Salem's Derby Street ferry landing. There are five departures daily during the May–October season, making Salem a very doable day trip from Boston for those without a car.

social justice themes with paintings that straddle the line between graffiti and fine art. You will be blown away.

The Peabody Essex Museum's historic house collection includes twenty-two structures—one of the largest collections of off-site properties of any museum in the country. Every major early American architectural style, including First Period, Georgian, and Federal, is represented within a three-block area of the Peabody Essex Museum's main campus in downtown Salem.

The *John Ward House* dates from 1684 and spans the First and Second Periods of colonial construction. Also called post-medieval style, the large timber-frame house has the distinctive deeply pitched gables, center chimney, and diamond-paned casement windows typical of the Puritan tradition. The John Ward House is directly across from the Peabody Essex Museum at 9 Brown Street and has been restored to a seventeenth-century aesthetic. It a wonderful example of what a Salem home would have looked like during the time of the witch trials.

It's a pleasant ten-minute walk along tree-lined brick sidewalks to Salem's McIntire Historic District, a largely residential area of Georgian and Federal period homes that were originally built for Salem's ruling merchant class. Many were designed by Samuel McIntire, one of America's first architects, who had his home and workshop in the neighborhood. The *Ropes Mansion* at 318 Essex Street is one of the grandest of the Georgian buildings; the nine-bedroom home was built in 1727 and is filled with a stunning array of original eighteenth- and nineteenth-century furnishings from four generations of the well-to-do Ropes family. You might recognize the Ropes Mansion from its cameo appearance as Alison's house in the 1993 Disney movie *Hocus Pocus*. Outside, the stunning one-acre Colonial Revival gardens are of a 1912 design and are impeccably maintained. The garden is open daily from dawn to dusk and is a favorite of the close-knit local community of dog owners. Admission to both the John Ward House and Ropes Mansion is free; they are generally open from late May through October on Saturday and Sunday from noon to 4 p.m.

Among the many program offerings and activities of the Salem Maritime National Historic Site (978-740-1650; nps.gov/sama), the *Derby Wharf National Recreational Trail* is often overlooked. It's a three-quarter-mile out-and-back walk; along the way you will pass *Friendship of Salem*, a replica of a 1797 square-rigged tall ship, and the 1770 Pedrick Store House. Your destination? Derby Light Station at the tip of the wharf—and very nearly out to sea. Established in 1871, it's a smallish lighthouse—just twenty feet tall and twelve feet square. Derby Light is still in use for navigation (although not open to the public). Originally whale-oil lamps were used; in recent years the lighthouse has been converted to solar power. Tip: Plan your walk before dawn to catch a spectacular sunrise over Salem Harbor.

Just around the corner from the harbor, at 48 Central Street, is one of the North Shore's best bakery/cafés. At breakfast, *A & J King Artisan Bakers* (978-744-4881; ajkingbakery.com) makes killer croissants and great egg, bacon, and cheese breakfast sandwiches. At lunch there are top-notch soups and salads, all served with toasted sourdough. Don't dare leave without picking up a chocolate chip cookie for later.

Another quick bite option? There are lots of great coffee shops in Salem, but for pure entertainment in this most eccentric of cities, snag a seat at *Jaho* (978-744-4300; jaho.com). It's a spacious, relaxing spot that is always buzzing with activity thanks to its waterfront location at 197 Derby Street on Pickering Wharf. If you need an option stronger than caffeine, this location also serves beer, wine, and cocktails.

The *Salem Witch Trials Memorial* (978-740-1250; voicesagainstinjustice .org) is the most low-key witch-related site in Salem, but it is the city's most significant step to address the legacy of the most painful moment in its history. Located in the center of town at 24 Liberty Street, the memorial was dedicated in 1992, three hundred years after the Salem Witch Trials. The space features twenty markers cantilevered along a low granite wall, each engraved with the name of one of the publicly executed victims. It's a solemn place for contemplation and meaningful conversation about disinformation, religious intolerance, and injustice.

Manchester-by-the-Sea

Is it Manchester or Manchester-by-the-Sea? It's actually both. Founded in 1645 as Manchester, the town officially changed its name in 1989 to avoid confusion with Manchester, New Hampshire, which is seventy miles to the north and very much inland. With its elegant sprawling homes around its picture-postcard harbor and adorable village, the town has always had a reputation of exclusivity—very much "coastal grandmother" before it was even a thing. And while signs and maps very clearly list the town as Manchester-by-the-Sea, locals always refer to their town simply as Manchester.

For one of the few Boston-area beaches accessible by public transportation, **Singing Beach** (978-526-7276; manchester.ma.us) is practically tourist-free. To reach this gorgeous spot, take the MBTA commuter rail to Manchester on the Newburyport/Rockport line, then walk a half mile up Beach Street. This seaside gem is renowned for the squeaking sound made when walking across the white sand. The half-mile-long beach has restrooms and a snack bar, and there is a small parking lot if you choose to drive. Walk-in fees are $10 per person (cash only) and are collected May through September.

Gloucester

Gloucester is having its moment. Again. Similar to the 2000 release of the blockbuster film *The Perfect Storm*, the city is experiencing a wave of interest after *CODA* won the 2022 best picture Oscar.

Just thirty miles north of Boston, Gloucester is America's oldest seaport. And for all its tourist allure, it is still a working waterfront that supports a fleet of sixty fishing boats. Gloucester has a longtime coexistence between working fishermen and working artists inspired by the sea. The **Cape Ann Museum** (978-283-0455; capeannmuseum.org) boasts a wonderful collection of fine art for a small regional institution. Edward Hopper, Childe Hassam, and Winslow Homer all spent summers painting in Gloucester, and the museum displays works from each. But the museum's strength is its collection of works by Gloucester-born Fitz Henry Lane—some forty romantic renderings of the Atlantic Ocean suffused with Cape Ann's luminous light. The museum is at 27 Pleasant Street and is open Tuesday through Saturday from 10 a.m. to 5 p.m. and Sunday from 1 to 4 p.m. Admission is $15 for adults and free for ages eighteen and under.

Across Gloucester Harbor, the **Rocky Neck Art Colony** (978-515-7004; rockyneckartcolony.org) at Smith Cove has been attracting artists since the 1850s and is considered the steward of Gloucester's plein air ("painting outdoors") legacy. Today Rocky Neck is a happening art enclave with a year-round cultural center, tons of galleries and eclectic boutiques, as well as a spate of new restaurants—in other words, Rocky Neck has the cool buzz that creatives bring to a neighborhood.

Set sail on the *Ardelle* (978-290-7168; maritimeheritagecharters.net), a hand-built Essex wooden schooner that offers two-hour public cruises of Gloucester Harbor from May through mid-October. A full-rigged clipper ship, *Ardelle* is a smaller, pinky schooner, meaning the vessel is pointed at both ends. *Ardelle's* design is very typical of nineteenth-century Cape Ann fishing boats—she is a stunning sight at full sail. Boarding is at 23 Harbor Loop Road. Tickets for adults are $45; $35 for children seventeen and under.

The path to **Salt Island** only appears with the ebb and flow of the sea— so timing is everything if you want to safely visit. Wooded and desolate, Salt Island is just offshore from Good Harbor Beach. Walk across the sandbar at low tide, and once on the island ascend the small hill to various open sections with views of Gloucester and the twin lighthouses at nearby Thatcher Island. The island is privately owned, but public access is allowed.

Rockport

Rockport is a tiny town, with a year-round population of some seven thousand residents. Like Gloucester, Rockport has a working waterfront. It also has a burgeoning reputation as an arts destination, with a thriving gallery scene as well as a unique regional concert venue.

For classical music lovers, the **Shalin Liu Performance Center** (978-546-7391; rockportmusic.org) is an under-the-radar stunner. The airy, sleekly modern concert hall fronts Main Street while also integrating its coastal surroundings, and has a stage that has as its backdrop a two-story glass window with views of the Atlantic Ocean. For audience members, it feels a little like being inside the bow of a ship. Yearly programming highlights include the Rockport Chamber Music Festival, Rockport Jazz Festival, and the Rockport Celtic Festival with a mix of local artists like pianist Marc-André Hamelin and out-of-town visitors like the Los Angeles Guitar Quartet, among others. It's an intimate space, with seating for just three hundred concertgoers, but it is just the right size for making live music a part of real life again.

A pair of islands make for a very happy day trip from Rockport. **Thatcher Island** (508-284-0144; thatcherisland.org), a mile off the coast, is home to twin

The Most Famous Fishing Shack in the World

At the end of Bearskin Neck, a simple red fishing shack on a granite pier watches over Rockport Harbor. It is known the world over as **Motif No. 1** and is said to be one of the most painted and, these days, most photographed landscapes in the world. What you see today is a replica—the original post-and-beam structure, built in the 1840s, was lost during the Blizzard of 1978. What's inside this most iconic of New England landmarks? It's used today just as was originally intended—as a space for local fishermen to store their gear.

pre-Revolutionary lighthouses, a small museum, a wildlife refuge, and three miles of wooded trails. It's only accessible by kayak or the Thatcher Island launch, which runs Wednesday and Saturday from June through August. The launch also makes a Tuesday run to *Straitsmouth Island* (978-887-9621; mass audubon.org), home to yet another historic lighthouse and a Massachusetts Audubon sanctuary with an ecosystem that supports an abundance of birds, including little blue herons and double-crested cormorants.

Swing by Rockport's *Paper House* (351-444-8931; paperhouserockport .com) on the way to Halibut Point State Park. The 1922 cottage is made entirely from newspaper. It's a one-of-a kind attraction and an example of upcycling at its finest. The house was designed and built by Elis Stenman, a mechanical engineer, with a wood foundation and roof. The walls, as well as all the furniture, are fashioned from newspaper that is bound with glue and varnished. Even after one hundred years, you can still read some of the headlines. The house is in a quiet residential neighborhood at 52 Pigeon Hill Street and is open spring through fall, daily from 1 p.m. to 5 p.m. Admission is by honesty box: $2 for adults and $1 for children. The house is unattended—just remember to close the door behind you.

trivia

Halibut Point has nothing to do with fish; rather the name comes from a sailing term, as mariners going around the tip of Cape Ann would need to change tack, or "haul about."

Just north of Rockport, you could easily pass *Halibut Point State Park* (978-546-2997; mass.gov/locations/halibut-point-state-park) if you are not keeping an eye out for it. Set your GPS for 4 Gott Avenue, just in case. The two-and-a-half-mile forested trail around the flooded abandoned granite quarry offers sweeping seascape views—on a clear day you can see the Isles of Shoals in New Hampshire and Maine's Mount Agamenticus. Granite was harvested from the quarry from the 1840s until 1929. Stand on the ridge overlooking the quarry and ponder the laborers slicing through the walls to remove the storied Rockport granite that built Boston's Longfellow Bridge and the Custom House Tower.

Essex

Just north of Rockport, the picturesque town of Essex is known for its ship-building heritage, its salt marsh, and its famous soft-shell clams. Essex is one of the best antiques towns in the state, with more than thirty distinctive shops up and down Main Street.

Essex has a long, intriguing history with the sea. The **Essex Historical Society and Shipbuilding Museum** (978-768-7541; essexshipbuilding .org) captures the town's 350 years of maritime history. Essex is famed for its wooden shipbuilding—four thousand boats were built by Essex shipwrights, many of them destined for the neighboring Gloucester fishing fleet. View a surviving 1927 schooner, the *Evelina M. Goulart*, and a maritime collection that includes ship models, paintings, and traditional ship-making tools. The shipyard is located on the town's historic waterfront site at 66 Main Street and is open daily from dawn to dusk for self-guided QR code tours. The museum is open Thursday to Sunday from 10 a.m. to 3 p.m. Admission is free, but donations are encouraged.

Messin' about on the river is best left to the professionals. **Essex River Cruises** (978-768-6981; essexcruises.com) offers small-boat cruises that are ideal for slow exploration. The Essex River is a magical place; it's home to spectacular scenery of small inlets, deserted islands, shifting sands, and seagrass as far as the eye can see. During the narrated ninety-minute cruise, you'll learn about the ecology of Essex Bay as well as the region's shipbuilding heritage. Essex River Cruises has a dock at 35 Dodge Street; regularly scheduled cruises take place daily from May through October. Fares for adults are $28; $16 for children age twelve and under.

Ipswich

Continue along State Route 1A to the small town of Ipswich, an agricultural community that boasts both stunning seascape and farmland as well as having colonial New England charm in spades. Ipswich has sixty known First Period (1625–1725) homes—more than any other place in the nation.

Straddling the Ipswich and Hamilton town lines, **Appleton Farms** (978-356-5728; thetrustees.org) dates from 1638 and is considered one of the oldest continually operating farms in the country. Appleton's one thousand acres are a perfectly pastoral setting of open meadows, forest, and miles of stone walls. There are endless walking options including six miles of hiking trails and another six miles of wide carriage lanes, known as "grass rides," that make for easy walking (and snowshoeing in winter). Appleton's "Old House" is beloved by the Ipswich community. It dates from 1794 and today, just as in the past, is the center of farm life and the farm's community programming. Don't leave without stopping by the terrific store, which features Appleton Farm produce and cheese made from milk supplied by the farm's herd of dairy cows. The farm's address is 219 County Road, and it is open year-round, daily from dawn to dusk. Admission is by parking fee: $6 on weekdays, $10 weekends.

There is always time for **White Farms Ice Cream** (978-356-2633) if you happen to be close by, most likely on a trip to or from Cranes Beach. This is a seasonal (March through October) cow-to-cone ice cream stand—all sixty flavors are made on the premises. They are particularly known for their peach ice cream, but they have all the old-school New England flavors covered as well, including maple walnut and black raspberry. White Farms is totally vintage; it's cash only. The address is 326 High Street, but you'll know you have arrived by the fiberglass cow on the roof.

"Bed-and-breakfast" does not do **The Inn at Castle Hill** (978-412-2555; theinnatcastlehill.com) justice. Originally built as a nineteenth-century farmhouse, the property was used as a summer cottage of the next-door Crane Estate Great House for much of the twentieth century. In 2000 the Trustees of Reservations Conservancy acquired the property and today manages it as a boutique hotel with ten sun-filled, beautifully appointed rooms. Gaze out at the estuary and Atlantic Ocean from the expansive front porch and plan your adventures: walking the estate's trails, exploring the gardens, or playing lawn games. It's an elevated guest experience that includes complimentary bicycles, passes to Crane Beach, a multicourse gourmet breakfast, and afternoon treats. The inn is open daily March through November, weekends only December through February.

Complete a bucket list of recreational activities at the Crane Estate, which encompasses not only the fifty-nine-bedroom Great House but also a 2,100-acre property that is essentially a playground for all kinds of year-round excitement. Kayaking? There are guided paddles of the Great Marsh or sunset kayak trips of the Crane Wildlife Refuge. Hiking? There are three-hour full-moon hikes on the dunes. Boating? Book a seat on a pontoon cruise of Essex Bay with a professional, seasoned birder. **Crane Outdoors** (978-356-3066; thetrustees.org) at 290 Argilla Road will set you up for each of these adventures and more.

Some of the fun that comes from visiting the **Clam Box of Ipswich** (978-3356-9707; clamboxofipswich.com) is just finding it. The restaurant's 1930s-era building at 246 High Street is shaped like a clam box and is a roadside attraction in its own right. The must-order are the whole-belly clams—a grease-drenched paper box of New England goodness.

Newburyport

Nestled between the Merrimack River and the Atlantic, Newburyport is a small harbor city that invites adventures in quiet places, including maritime forests, the Great Salt Marsh, and small bays and inlets where nature reigns. You can almost hear the whisper of clippers ships in the revitalized historic downtown, which also has a happening dining scene.

Take State Route 1A north to Plum Island, an eleven-mile-long barrier island that lies halfway between Newbury and Newburyport. Access to the island is via a causeway, the Plum Island Turnpike, and across a drawbridge over the Plum Island River. The *Parker River National Wildlife Refuge* (978-465-5753; fws.gov/refuge/parker-river) is a US Fish and Wildlife Service property that encompasses nearly two-thirds of the island. The island is a prime birding spot; its location sits along the Atlantic Flyway, a major north–south migratory pathway. Walking trails weave through woods and along the shore. Large stretches of boardwalk allow visitors to easily cross the tidal estuaries— it's a wonderful place to watch the grebes dive for small fish. Check in at the visitor center at 6 Plum Island Turnpike to pay the vehicle day pass fee of $6. From here you can drive the length of the island along Refuge Road. There are multiple parking lots along the way to access the various walking trails and the beach. The refuge is open daily from sunrise to sunset; the visitor center is open daily from 9 a.m. to 4 p.m.

If you want to get to know Massachusetts, get to know its state parks. *Maudslay State Park* (978-465-7223; mass.gov/locations/maudslay state -park) is a prime example of one of the state's best. Located on the banks of the Merrimack River, what was once a nineteenth-century 480-acre estate offers exceptional scenery. As you wander the dreamy grounds, you'll spot plenty of birds among the thickets of pine, laurel, and beech. Only the ruins of the main house remain, but the formal gardens and are kept in bloom from late spring through September and are sure to inspire. The carriage way trails are easy and serene, snaking through the woods, across open fields, and over a three-arch stone bridge. The entrance to the park is at 74 Curzon Mill Road, and it is open daily year-round from dawn to dusk. Admission is by parking fee: $5 for Massachusetts residents, $20 for nonresidents.

A comprehensive collection of all things seafaring can be found at the *Custom House Maritime Museum* (978-462-8681; customhousemaritime museum.org). View artifacts of distant voyages that span the seventeenth to twentieth centuries, including paintings, scientific instruments, uniforms, and intricate ship models. Unique to this maritime museum is its focus on the connection between the US Coast Guard and Newburyport. The museum has a prime harbor location at 25 Water Street in an 1835 Greek Revival building that was Newburyport's former customhouse. From May through September the museum is open Tuesday, Wednesday, and Sunday from noon to 4 p.m.; Thursday through Saturday from 10 a.m. to 5 p.m. October through April, hours are Thursday to Saturday 10 a.m. to 4 p.m. and Sunday noon to 4 p.m.

Continuing north along State Route 1A is the town of Amesbury, a seacoast city of about sixteen thousand that is practically within spitting distance of the New Hampshire state line. ***Lowell's Boat Shop*** (978-834-0050; lowells boatshop.com), established in 1793, is the oldest continually operating boat shop in America. The shop is a National Historic Landmark and a working museum. During its heyday in the late 1800s, Amesbury fishing dories were renowned up and down the East Coast for their seaworthiness. What is a dory? A dory is a rowing boat, used on schooners for fishing cod and haddock. The Amesbury dory's simple design featured a flat bottom, high sides, and a sharp bow and stern that could be easily replicated. The shop still handcrafts dories and skiffs while teaching the art to the next generation of boatbuilders. On the main floor, visitors can watch the process, as several boats are typically under construction at any given time. Be sure to stop in the basement, which was historically the paint room. Today it tells the story of the region's shipbuilding roots. Lowell's Boat Shop is located on the banks of the Merrimack River at 459 Main Street and is open for walk-in tours Tuesday through Friday 11 a.m. to 4 p.m. and Saturday 10 a.m. to 3 p.m. Guided tours are $8; self-guided tours are $5.

Lowell

It's a lovely drive in the country along State Route 133 West to Lowell. Located on the Merrimac River, Lowell is named for Francis Cabot Lowell, a Newburyport-born merchant who pioneered the idea of a factory system that integrated labor along with a planned industrial city to accommodate the large workforce needed to run the mills.

In the late 1800s Lowell was a pioneering city, leading the country into the industrial era with its water-powered textile mills. "Spindle City" has mills and more mills, a canal-carved downtown, and classic redbrick architecture. Lowell is a city that thrives on reinvention and is forever making a comeback.

Time has marched past Lowell's defining moment as the country's center for textile manufacturing, but it is not hard to imagine the din of a room full of steam-powered working looms and the eighty young women who made the machines run at the ***Lowell National Historical Park*** (978-970-5000; nps .gov/lowe). To operate the looms, mill owners recruited young women from local farm families or from Canada—and were able to pay them less than men for their labor. The Morgan Cultural Center focuses on the lives of the Mill Girls, as they came to be known, who toiled as many as twelve hours a day turning cotton into cloth. Spread across downtown Lowell, this is an urban National Park Service site offering a variety of experiences. Ranger-narrated

The Art of James McNeill Whistler

Fun fact: The painter James McNeill Whistler was born in Lowell in 1834. Whistler's most famous work is *Arrangement in Grey and Black No. 1* — the painting better known as *Whistler's Mother*. Whistler's mother did indeed sit for the portrait. The painting was the first work by an American artist that was purchased by France; originally displayed in the Louvre, it now makes its home at Paris's Musee D'Orsay. The **Whistler House Museum of Art** (978-452-7641; whistlerhouse.org) is the home of the Lowell Art Association, which lovingly maintains the birthplace of one of their own while promoting the work of the next generation of Lowell artists through special exhibits. The museum has a very good reproduction of *Whistler's Mother* to view and a gallery of Whistler's etchings, as well as a sketches by John Singer Sargent (Whistler and Sargent were friends). Also be sure to check out the stunning bronze sculpture of Whistler in the little park across the street by Tewksbury artist Mico Kaufman. The museum is open Wednesday through Saturday from 11 a.m. to 4 p.m. Admission is $12 for adults and $5 for children age twelve and under. The address is in the center of downtown, between the Lowell Historic Park and the Quilt Museum at 243 Worthen Street.

(the very best kind) ninety-minute boat tours of Lowell's working canal and lock system are a highlight of a visit—there is limited seating, so make reservations online in advance. The park is open daily 10 a.m. to 5 p.m. The visitor center is at 246 Market Street and should be your first stop. The Boott Cotton Mills Museum houses the looms and is a short walk away on the river at 115 John Street. Museum admission is $6 for adults, $3 for ages six through sixteen. Canal Boat tours are $12 for adults and $8 for children ages six through fifteen, free for age five and under.

The **New England Quilt Museum** (978-452-4207; neqm.org) is a fitting counterpoint between Lowell's textile history and the city's thriving artistic community. This is the second-oldest quilt museum in the country and offers a captivating collection of some five hundred pieces that span three centuries of quilt making in America, including traditional, contemporary, and studio art quilts.

trivia

Lowell's other most famous son is writer Jack Kerouac, who was born in 1922 to French-Canadian parents in a modest double-decker in the city's Centralville neighborhood. While his 1957 coming-of-age novel, *On the Road*, was based on his travels across America, five of his other books were set in his working-class hometown. The city celebrates Kerouac's legacy with a memorial at Kerouac Park on Bridge and French Streets that features a series of granite columns etched with excerpts from his writings.

After touring the collection, you'll likely have a newfound appreciation for the variety, creativity, and craftmanship of quilts and quilting, an art form that traditionally has been the work of women artists. The museum is part of the Canalway Cultural District at 18 Shattuck Street and is open Tuesday through Saturday from 10 a.m. to 4 p.m. Admission is $9.

Places to Stay North of Boston

ESSEX

Shea's Riverside Inn & Motel
132 Main St.
(978) 768-6800
sheasinn.com

GLOUCESTER

Beauport Hotel Gloucester
55 Commercial St.
(978) 282-0008
beauporthotel.com

Harborview Inn
71 Western Ave.
(978) 283-2277
harborviewinn.com

IPSWICH

Rogers and Brown House
83 Country Rd.
(978) 356-9600
rogersandbrownhouse.com

LOWELL

Sonesta Select
30 Industrial Ave.
(800) 766-3782
sonesta.com

NEWBURYPORT

Compass Rose Inn
5½ Center St.
(978) 673-0826
compassrosenewburyport.com

Essex Street Inn
7 Essex St.
(978) 465-3148
essexstreetinn.com

Garrison Inn Boutique Hotel
11 Brown Square
(978) 499-8500
garrisoninn.com

ROCKPORT

Addison Choate
49 Broadway St.
(978) 546-7543
addisonchoate.com

Emerson Inn
1 Cathedral Ave.
(978) 546-6321
theemersoninn.com

Sally Webster Inn
34 Mount Pleasant St.
(978) 390-8159
sallywebster.com

SALEM

Hawthorne Hotel
18 Washington Square West
(978) 647-2780
hawthornehotel.com

Hotel Salem
209 Essex St.
(978) 306-4050
larkhotels.com

Morning Glory Bed and Breakfast
22 Hardy St.
(978) 741-1703
morningglorybb.com

Northey Street House Bed and Breakfast
30 Northey St.
(978) 397-1582
northeystreethouse.com

Salem Waterfront Hotel and Suites
225 Derby St.
(978) 306-4358
salemwaterfronthotel.com

Places to Eat North of Boston

ESSEX

CK Pearl
112 Main St.
(978) 890-7378
ckpearl.com
American

Rivers Bend
35 Dodge St.
(978) 890-7098
riversbend.com
American

Woodman's of Essex
119 Main St.
(978) 768-6451
woodmans.com
Seafood

GLOUCESTER

Lobsta Land
84 Causeway St.
(978) 281-0415
lobstalandrestaurant.com
Seafood

Passports
110 Main St.
(978) 281-3680
passportsrestaurant.com
World cuisine

Short & Main
36 Main St.
(978) 281-0044
Shortandmain.com
Pizza/Italian

Sugar Magnolia's
112 Main St.
(978) 281-5310
sugarmags.com
Breakfast

Talise
33 River Rd.
(978) 515-7814
taliserestaurant.com
New American

IPSWICH

Choate Bridge Restaurant
3 S. Main St.
(978) 356-2931
choatebridgepub.com
Seafood/pub

Hart House 1640
51 Linebrook Rd.
(978) 356-1640
1640harthouse.com
New England

Ithaki
25 Hammatt St
(978) 356-0099
ithakicuisine.com
Greek

OTHER ATTRACTIONS

Cape Ann Whale Watch
415 Main St.
Gloucester
(978) 283-5110
seethewhales.com

Castle Hill on the Crane Estate
290 Argilla Rd.
Ipswich
(978) 356-4351
thetrustees.org

House of Seven Gables
115 Derby St.
Salem
(978) 744-0991
7gables.org

Peabody Essex Museum
161 Essex St.
Salem
(978) 745-9500
pem.org

Salem Maritime National Historic Site
2 New Liberty St.
Salem
(978) 740-1650
nps.gov/sama

LOWELL

Four Sisters Owl Diner
244 Appleton St.
(978) 453-8321
theowldiner.com
Breakfast/lunch

Life Alive Organic Café
194 Middle St.
(978) 453-1311
Lifealive.com
Coffee/vegetarian

Mill City BBQ and Brew
1018 Gorham St.
(978) 614-0156
millcitybarbecue.com
Barbecue

Pho 88
1270 Westford St.
(978) 452-7300
pho88online.net
Vietnamese

NEWBURY

Bob's Lobster
49 Plum Island Turnpike
(978) 465-7100
boblobster.com
Seafood

Sunset Club
4 Old Point Rd.
sunsetclubpi.com
Beachside bar

NEWBURYPORT

Bar 25
38 State St.
(978) 255-3322
bar-25.com
Mediterranean/Middle
Eastern

Loretta
15 Pleasant St.
(978) 463-0000
lorettarestaurant.com
New American

Metzy's
5 Boston Way
(978) 255-7347
metzys.com
Mexican

Port City Sandwich Company
40 Merrimack St.
(978) 358-8628
Portcitysandwichco.com
Sandwiches

Stone Crust Pizza
8 Pleasant St.
(978) 462-2015
stonecrustpizza.com
Pizza

SELECTED CHAMBERS OF COMMERCE & TOURISM BUREAUS

Destination Salem
81 Washington St.
Salem 01970
(800) 322-1128
salem.org

Discover Gloucester
PO Box 915
Gloucester 01930
(978) 675-1818
discovergloucester.com

Greater Cape Ann Chamber of Commerce
24 Harbor Loop
Gloucester 01930
(978) 283-1601
capeannvacations.com

Greater Lowell Chamber of Commerce
133 Merrimack St.
Lowell 01852
(978) 459-8154
greaterlowellcc.org

North of Boston Convention and Visitors Bureau
Exit 6
Salisbury 01952
(978) 465-6555
northofboston.org

Tuscan Sea Grill & Bar
38R Merrimac St.
(978) 465-2211
Tuscanseagrillbar.com
Seafood

ROCKPORT

Feather & Wedge
5 Main St.
(978) 999-5917
featherandwedge.com
New American

Heath's Tea Room
43 South St.
(978) 309-3388
heathstearoom.com
Tearoom/lunch

Hula Moon
27 Mount Pleasant St.
(978) 546-2572
Breakfast/lunch

Lobster Pool
329 Granite St.
(978) 546-7808
thelobsterpool.com
Seafood

Roy Moore Lobster
39 Bearskin Neck
(978) 546-6696
Seafood

SALEM

Bambolina
288 Derby St.
(978) 594-8709
bambolinarestaurant.com
Pizza

**Caramel French
Patisserie**
281 Essex St.
(978) 594-0244
French bakery

Goodnight Fatty
1 Washington Square
(978) 822-2277
goodnightfatty.com
Cookies

Ledger
125 Washington St.
(978) 594-1908
ledgersalem.com
New American

Red's Sandwich Shop
15 Central St.
(978) 745-3527
redskitchenandtavern.com
Breakfast/sandwiches

Turners Seafood
43 Church St.
(978) 745-7665
turnersseafood.com
Seafood

South of Boston

Geographically, the area considered "south of Boston" is huge. It includes not only the slice of Massachusetts coast known as the South Shore, which extends just past Boston along State Route 3 to Cape Cod (basically all of Plymouth County), but also Norfolk and Bristol Counties in the southeastern part of the state. Highlights include Milton, a classic New England bedroom community; Quincy, the birthplace of two of the country's earliest presidents (John Adams and his son John Quincy Adams); Plymouth, which thrives on its ties to the first Thanksgiving; New Bedford, an important seventeenth-century whaling port; and a handful of charming New England inland towns in between.

Milton

While driving south from Boston, notice that Adams Street runs seven miles through the city's Dorchester neighborhood and into the towns of Milton and Quincy. Milton's proximity to Boston keeps it a culturally diverse city, but it is also particularly bucolic, as it is home to the seven-thousand-acre Blue Hills Reservation.

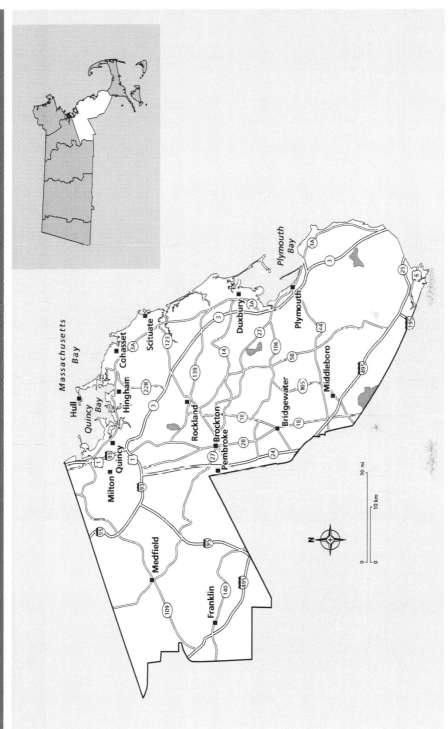

Massachusetts
Bay

Plymouth
Bay

Plymouth

Duxbury

Scituate

Cohasset

Hull

Quincy
Bay

Hingham

Rockland

Brockton

Pembroke

Bridgewater

Middleboro

Quincy

Milton

Medfield

Franklin

N

10 mi

10 km

Roadside historians may want to pop in at the **Forbes House Museum** (617-696-1815; forbeshousemuseum.org) at 215 Adams Street, a Greek Revival mansion that dates from 1833. Beautifully sited on a hillcrest overlooking the Neponset marsh with a view of both Boston Harbor and the city skyline, the home was built by Robert Bennet Forbes, a sea captain and China Trade merchant, for his mother, Margaret Perkins Forbes. Guided tours focus on the home's many fine examples of export works of art. The estate's grounds feature an exact replica of the Kentucky cabin where Abraham Lincoln was born. The museum is open Friday through Sunday from 10 a.m. to 3 p.m.; admission is $10 for adults, $8 for students.

trivia

Travel out of Boston along the Southeast Expressway (Interstate 93) toward Dorchester and be on the lookout for the giant rainbow painted on a 150-foot-high natural-gas tank. Commissioned in 1971 by Boston Gas, the work known as *Rainbow Swash* was painted by pop artist/nun/teacher/activist Corita Kent and is one of the largest copyrighted works of art in the world. Some say that the profile of Vietnamese leader Ho Chi Minh can be seen in the blue stripe.

When it comes to weather tracking, the **Blue Hills Observatory** (617-696-0562; bluehill.org) is tops. Located within Blue Hills Reservation, the 635-foot stone weather tower dates from 1885 and is home to the longest continuously running daily weather records from one site in all of North America. To reach the observatory, you will need to hike one mile to the summit from the parking lot at 1 Observatory Service Road—but what a view! On a clear day you can see the mountains of Vermont to the north and Mount Wachusett to the west. The tower is open Saturday and Sunday from 10 a.m. to 4 p.m.; admission is $4 for adults and $2 for children.

The **Blue Hills Trailside Museum** serves as Massachusetts Audubon's Boston sanctuary and is just the right size for families with young children. Indoor exhibits focus on smaller animals like rattlesnakes and snowy owls, while outdoors you will find native wildlife, including deer, red foxes, eagles, and everyone's favorite—playful, fun-loving river otters. The parking lot address is 1904 Canton Avenue, and it is a great stepping-off point for the 125 miles of trails of the Blue Hills Reservation. The museum is open Wednesday through Sunday from 9 a.m. to 4 p.m.; admission is $5 for adults, $3 for children.

Quincy

If you are a colonial American history enthusiast, the town of Quincy is a must-visit. The "City of Presidents" is the birthplace of two US presidents: second president John Adams and sixth President John Quincy Adams, as well as John Hancock, president of the Continental Congress (it was in this capacity that Hancock was the first person to sign the Declaration of Independence). By the early 1800s, what was once a small agricultural and fishing village became a boomtown with the development of the granite and, later, shipbuilding industries.

Adam's National Historical Park (617-773-1117; nps.gov/adam/index .htm) encompasses several sites that relate to four generations of the Adams family, including the birth homes of both John Adams and John Quincy Adams; the family estate Peace Field, also known as The Old House; and the Stone Library, which holds much of the family's books and papers. Guided tours of the park include trolley transportation between the sites; tours typically take two and a half to three hours, with time to wander the gardens and grounds. The visitor center is located at 1250 Hancock Street and has a garage that offers validated parking. It operates year-round for screening an introductory film and is also the starting point for the seasonal trolley. The homes are open May through October, Wednesday through Sunday from 9 a.m. to 5 p.m. Admission is $15 for adults, free for ages sixteen and under.

Not far away, at 1306 Hancock Street, the Adams's family crypt is tucked in the subterranean level of the ***United First Parish Church*** (617-773-1290; ufpc.org) and is the final resting place of both presidents. Dating from 1639, and originally Puritan, the congregation became Unitarian in 1750 and was the parish church of the Adams family. Historic tours of the church and crypt are offered Monday, Tuesday, and Thursday through Saturday from 11 a.m. to 4 p.m. and on Sunday from noon to 4 p.m. Suggested donation is $5 for adults.

For a quick lunch, check out ***Rubato*** (617-481-2049; rubato-food.com) at 412 Hancock Street. Chef Laurence Louie showcases a passion for modern Hong Kong cuisine like baos and congee, but the star here is the fried chicken bolo sandwich with sesame slaw. Another easy option in Quincy Center is ***Craig's Café*** (617-770-9271; craigscafe.com) at 1354 Hancock Street for a solid menu of burgers, wraps, and sandwiches.

Quincy's proud shipbuilding heritage is on full display at the ***United States Naval Shipbuilding Museum*** (617-479-7900; uss-salem.org) located in Quincy's fabled Fore River Shipyard.

trivia

Quincy is also the birthplace of Dunkin' Donuts—now simply named Dunkin'. Founded in 1948, the shop is still in operation at 543 Southern Artery. The shop has had a recent refresh that features a retro design: a horseshoe-shaped counter, vinyl stool seating, and vintage signage. All the classics are here too, including Boston Kreme, Blueberry Cake, and Chocolate Frosted.

The centerpiece attraction is the USS *Salem*, a heavy cruiser completed at the end of World War II.

She never saw combat but served as a flagship for the US Navy in the Mediterranean until the late 1950s. Like a lot of military museums, the volunteers have a wealth of institutional knowledge from their own time in the service and enjoy sharing their passion with visitors—you may very well find yourself treated to a near-private tour. It's hard to miss the hulking ship in the harbor; 549 South Street is the address for Pier 3. The museum is open April through June and September through November, Saturday and Sunday from 10 a.m. to 4 p.m. During July and August, the museum is open Friday through Sunday from 10 a.m. to 4 p.m. Admission is $12 for adults and $10 for children.

Hingham, Hull, and Scituate

Visitors to the Cape often bypass these three neighboring coastal towns that lie midway between Boston and Plymouth—and that's perfectly fine with locals, who enjoy their quiet villages and breathtaking beaches without roads filled with day-tripping tourists. This part of the South Shore is known as the "Irish Riviera" because of its large Irish American population; the region is full of Irish pubs, from cozy spots where you can take your nan to dive bars for a quiet pint alone.

Just off State Route 3A, in a residential Hingham neighborhood, **World's End** (781-740-7233; thetrustees.org/place/worlds-end-hingham) is seemingly just that—a 250-acre spit of conservation land that juts out into Hingham Harbor with views of the Boston skyline and Nantasket Beach. The property features more than four miles of walking trails through woods and marsh and along the shore and is open daily from 8 a.m. to sunset. Admission is $8 weekends, $6 weekdays; pay at the guardhouse at Martin's Lane.

In Hingham Square, at 116 North Street, the **Snug** (781-749-9774; snugpub .com) is beloved locally as a place for a chat and a brew. The menu is all about New England classics and Irish fare: fish-and-chips, shepherd's pie, and steak tips. The Snug also has a long-running traditional sessiun on Monday evenings that's worth making dinner plans around.

The **Hull Lifesaving Museum** (781-925-5433; lifesavingmuseum.org) is a terrific stop after a day at the beach. Located in 1889 in a lifesaving station that was operated by the US Coast Guard and its precursor, the US Life-Saving Service, the museum overlooks Boston Harbor and has a view of Boston Light (the country's oldest lighthouse) from its front porch. The museum commemorates the brave rescuers who saved countless shipwrecked crews from the rocky coast and shoals of Boston Harbor during the seventeenth and eighteenth centuries. Fascinating artifacts include vintage lifesaving equipment, treasure salvaged from shipwrecks, and the 1887 surfboat Nantasket. The museum is located at 1117 Nantasket Avenue and is open Monday and Thursday from 10 a.m. to 2 p.m. and Friday through Sunday from 10 a.m. to 4 p.m. Over at the Windmill Point boathouse, the museum sponsors open-water rowing lessons and races.

The charmingly quaint *Maritime and Irish Mossing Museum* (781-545-5565; scituatehistoricalsociety.org) offers a fascinating look at the Irish moss industry and its impact on South Shore immigration. What is Irish moss, exactly? It's carrageen, or red algae, a common natural thickening agent used in cooking. In 1850 David Ward, a local Irish immigrant, realized that the seaweed was abundant in South Shore waters and saw an opportunity. By the 1870s, one hundred Irish families had settled in Scituate to work in what was then a booming moss industry. The museum, located at 301 Driftway Road, is part of the Scituate Historical Society and is open on Sunday from 1 p.m. to 4 p.m. Admission is $5.

Just down the road, *Hummarock Beach* (781-545-8700; scituatema.gov) is an under-the-radar South Shore gem—a three-mile barrier island with terrain that consists of soft sand, dune grass, and a bit of cobble. Come early (or late) to snag one on the public parking spaces along Marshfield Avenue.

Scituate can make for a good, less-expensive beach getaway than pricier Cape Cod. With a picturesque waterfront location, the *Inn at Scituate Harbor* (781-545-5550; innatscituate.com) offers twenty-nine quintessentially New England guest rooms inspired by the nautical culture of the South Shore. Rooms are decorated in ocean shades, many have decks, and all rates include a continental breakfast. The inn is at 8 Beaver Sam Road.

Duxbury's *Art Complex Museum* (781-934-6634; artcomplex.org) is an unexpected haven of stellar art in this quiet coastal hamlet. Opened in 1971, this intimate museum set on thirteen acres of woods houses the art collection of the Carl A. Weyerhaeuser family. The museum's works by John Singer Sargent, Childe Hassam, and Mary Cassatt would make any big American city proud, but its Asian collection is just as exceptional, with paintings, ceramics, and bronzes dating from the prehistoric to the present. The museum is located at 189 Alden Street and is open Wednesday through Sunday from 1 p.m. to 4 p.m. Admission is free.

Plymouth

Continue heading south along State Route 3 to Plymouth, forever tied to the story of the events that led to the first Thanksgiving. At *Plimoth Patuxet*

The Cranberry Highway

The section of State Route 28 that stretches thirty miles from Plymouth to Wareham is known as the "Cranberry Highway." Centuries-old cranberry bogs dot this entire region, and in September and October, traveling past fields, farms, and marshes reveals a stunning sight: a sea of crimson cranberries against a backdrop of yellow and orange autumn foliage. The Cape Cod Cranberry Growers' Association is based in Plymouth and represents the state's cranberry farmers; check their website (cranberries.org) for information regarding seasonal harvest tours.

Museums (508-746-1622; plimoth.org), the past is anything but musty. The outdoor living history museum features costumed reenactors who portray life in a re-creation of Plimoth, the village founded by the Pilgrims who arrived here in 1620 on the *Mayflower*. Native Wampanoag interpreters showcase indigenous cooking and farming methods as well as cultural practices at the Patuxet homesite, which features a large thatched house, or wetu. Engage with the guides, then head over to Plymouth Harbor to see *Mayflower II*—a full-scale replica of the Pilgrims' vessel and a testament to the skill of shipbuilders past and present. The museum's campus address is 137 Warren Street. The museum is open daily from late April through November; hours are 9 a.m. to 5 p.m. Admission is $42.50 for adults, $27.50 for children; single admission tickets for either the village or *Mayflower II* are available as well.

Directly on the harbor at 15 Town Pier, **Wood's Seafood** (508-746-0261; woodsseafood.com) has a water-view patio and serves an excellent lobster roll and fried seafood within walking distance of *Mayflower II*.

After a full day of history, wind down at **Plymouth Bay Winery** (508-746-2100; plymouthbaywinery.com), which goes beyond the grape with its many wines made from locally grown fruit. In business for twenty years, Plymouth Bay is mostly known for their handcrafted Cranberry Blush, which has a fresh berry aroma and a tart, tannic complexity. Other offerings are refreshing pear-, apricot-, and blueberry-based wines—each pairs well with vodka or makes a marvelous spritz. The winery is across from the harbor at 114 Water Street and conveniently has a large parking lot. Tastings are offered daily (no reservation necessary) and you get to keep the glass as a souvenir.

New Bedford

The seaport city of New Bedford was the world capital of the whaling industry in the 1820s and has been immortalized in Herman Melville's *Moby-Dick* as "perhaps the dearest place to live, in all New England." Today, New Bedford is a city made for strolling, with narrow cobblestone streets, historic homes, landmark buildings, and a deep harbor with a working fishing fleet at anchor.

Uncover the story of "the city that lit the world" at the **New Bedford Whaling National Historic Park** (508-996-4095; nps.gov/nebe), a unique public-private partnership that preserves and interprets New Bedford's whaling history. The ranger-led walking tours are exceptional. Retrace the steps of New Bedford's seamen in their pursuit of whales on ever-longer voyages around the globe, as well as learn about the city's significant role as a haven for fugitive slaves in the years leading up to the Civil War. The visitor center is at 33 William Street; hours are Wednesday through Sunday from 10 a.m. to 4 p.m. Admission is free.

Suspended from the ceiling of the **New Bedford Whaling Museum** (508-997-0046; whalingmuseum.org), Kobo is a 66-foot blue whale skeleton that sets the tone for exhibits that explore the history of New Bedford's whaling industry and the importance of conservation. The museum's collection of scrimshaw art—intricate whalebone etchings and carvings—is impressive. And don't miss the opportunity to step aboard the *Lagoda*, a spectacular half-size 1915 model of a whaling ship—one of the largest ship models in the world. The museum is at 18 Johnny Cake Hill and is open daily from 9 a.m. to 5 p.m.; admission is $19 for adults, $9 for children.

Twenty miles south of Boston, drive along scenic State Route 24 to Brockton. **The Fuller Craft Museum** (508-588-6000) is all about contemporary handmade objets d'art, from sublime burnished-metal jewelry, to eye-catching glass mosaics, to basketry in a range of materials. The museum is a local institution that sets itself apart with its creative programming, family-friendliness, and community spirit. The museum's address is 455 Oak Street; the campus also includes an outdoor sculpture garden and is open Tuesday through Sunday from 10 a.m. to 5 p.m. Admission is by suggested donation of $12.

An Unlikely Story Bookstore & Café (508-699-0244; anunlikelystory .com) is the very definition of a destination bookstore. The operative word being "destination," since the shop is in the small town of Plainville in the extreme southeast corner of the state. Parents of reluctant readers will likely

trivia

Massachusetts is not only the birthplace of the nation but also of chocolate chip cookies. Whitman's Ruth Graves Wakefield created the treat at her Toll House Inn restaurant in 1938 when she broke up a bar of semisweet chocolate to add to her drop cookie recipe. Toll House chocolate chip cookies became an instant hit and were recognized as the official Massachusetts state cookie in 1997.

know the work of the store's owner well; Jeff Kinney, author of *The Diary of a Wimpy Kid*, lives nearby with his family. The store is expansive, selling both children's and mainstream titles. A bookstore that is as much about community as books, it is also home to both a second-floor event space and a café. The store's address is 111 South Street.

AUTHOR'S TOP TEN PICKS

Adam's National Historical Park
135 Adams St.
Quincy
(617) 773-1117
nps.gov/adam/index.htm

Art Complex Museum
189 Alden St.
Duxbury
(781) 934-6634
artcomplex.org

Blue Hills Trailside Museum
1904 Canton Ave.
Milton
(617) 333-0690
www.massaudubon.org

Fuller Craft Museum
455 Oak St.
Brockton
(508) 588-6000
fullercraft.org

Hull Lifesaving Museum
1117 Nantasket Ave.
Hull
(781) 925-5433
hulllifesavingmuseum.org

Maritime and Irish Mossing Museum
301 Driftway Rd.
Scituate
(781) 545-5565
scituatehistoricalsociety.org

New Bedford Whaling Museum
18 Johnny Cake Hill
New Bedford
(508) 997-0046
whalingmuseum.org

Plimoth Patuxet Museums (and *Mayflower II*)
137 Warren St.
Plymouth
(508)746-1622
plimoth.org

United States Naval Shipbuilding Museum
549 South St., Pier 3
Quincy
(617) 479-7900
uss-salem.org

World's End
Martin's Lane
Hingham
(781) 740-7233
thetrustees.org/place/
worlds-end-hingham

Places to Stay South of Boston

COHASSET

Red Lion Inn
71 S. Main St.
(781) 383-1704
hotel1620.com

HULL

Beacon Waterfront Inn
52 Salisbury St.
(781) 528-0627
beaconhull.com

Nantasket Beach Hotel
115 Nantasket Ave.
(339) 218-3342
nantaskethotel.com

Nantasket Beach Resort
45 Hull Shore Dr.
(855) 992-3383
nantasketbeachresort.com

MATTAPOISETT

The Inn on Shipyard Park
13 Water St.
(508) 758-4922
theinnonthepark.com

NEW BEDFORD

New Bedford Harbor Hotel
222 Union St.
(508) 999-1292
newbedfordharborhotel.com

Whalehouse
100 Madison St.
(339) 832-3123
thewhalehousenb.com

PLYMOUTH

Hotel 1620
180 Water St.
(508) 747-4900
hotel1620.com

Mirabeau Inn & Spa
35 Landmark Dr.
(844) 255-9828
plymouthmirbeau.com

QUINCY

Best Western Adams Inn Quincy-Boston
29 Hancock St.
(617) 328-1500
bwadamsinn.com

SCITUATE

Inn at Scituate Harbor
8 Beaver Dam Rd.
(781) 545-5550
innatscituate.com

TOP ANNUAL EVENTS

JANUARY

Moby-Dick Marathon
New Bedford
(508) 987-0046
whalingmuseum.org

AUGUST

Portuguese Feast of the Blessed Sacrament
New Bedford
(508) 992-6691
feastoftheblessedsacramentcom.ning.com

Marshfield Fair
Marshfield
(781) 834-6629
marshfieldfair.org

NOVEMBER

America's Hometown Thanksgiving Celebration
Plymouth
(508) 746-1818
usathanksgiving.com

Cranfest
Plymouth
(508) 746-1622
plimoth.org

Places to Eat South of Boston

COHASSET

Olde Salt House
44 Border St.
(781) 383-0900
oldesalthousecohasset
.com
Seafood

HINGHAM

Scarlet Oak Tavern
1217 Main St.
(781) 749-8200
scarletoaktavern.com
New England

Tosca
14 North St.
(781) 740-0080
toscahingham.com
Italian

MILTON

Abby Park
550 Adams St.
(617) 696-8700
abbypark.com
American bistro

Newcomb Farms Restaurant
1139 Randolph Ave.
(617) 698-9547
newcombfarmsrestaurant
.com
Breakfast/lunch

Novara
556 Adams St.
(617) 696-8400
novararestaurant.com
Italian

Steel & Rye
95 Eliot St.
(617) 690-2787
steelandrye.com
Bakery/New American

NEW BEDFORD

Antonio's
267 Coggeshall St.
(508) 903-636
antoniosnewbedford.com
Portuguese

Black Whale
Fisherman's Wharf, Pier 3
(508) 990-7100
theblackwhale.com

OTHER ATTRACTIONS

Blue Hills Reservation
725 Hillside St.
Milton
(617) 698-1802
mass.gov/locations/blue-hills-reservation

Buttonwood Park Zoo
425 Hawthorn St.
New Bedford
(508) 991-6178
bpzoo.org

Children's Museum Easton
9 Sullivan Ave.
North Easton
(508) 230-3789
cmeaston.org

Nantasket Beach
212 Nantasket Ave.
Hull
(781) 925-1777
mass.gov/locations/
nantasket-beach-reservation

Plymouth Rock
79 Water St.
Plymouth
(508) 747-5360
mass.gov/locations/
pilgrim-memorial-state-park

Horseneck State Beach Reservation
5 John Reed Rd.
Westport
(508) 636-8816
mass.gov/locations/
horseneck-beach-state-reservation

SELECTED CHAMBERS OF COMMERCE & TOURISM BUREAUS

Destination New Bedford
133 William St.
New Bedford 02740
(508) 979-1745
destinationnewbedford.org

Discover Quincy
1305 Hancock St.
Quincy 02169
(617) 376-1110
discoverquincy.com

See Plymouth Tourism
4 North St.
Plymouth 02360
(508) 747-0100
seeplymouth.com

Brick Pizzeria Napoletana
163 Union St.
(508) 999-4943
Pizzeriabrick.com
Pizza

Moby Dick Brewing Company
16 South Water St.
(774) 202-6961
mobydickbrewing.com
American

PLYMOUTH

Cork & Table
23 Court St.
(774) 454-3683
corkandtableplymouth.com
American

Rye Tavern Plymouth
517 Old Sandwich Rd.
(508) 591-7515
theryetavern.com
Farm-to-table

QUINCY

Alba
1486 Hancock St.
(617) 376-2522
albaquincy.com
Steak & Seafood

Fat Cat
1495 Hancock St.
(617) 471-4363
American

The Townshend
1250 Hancock St.
(617) 481-9649
thetownshend.com
American

Cape Cod

Cape Cod is a fabled New England summer destination. The seventy-mile-long peninsula is shaped like a bent arm, making a fist as it flexes into the Atlantic. The region is home to sweeping beaches, historic lighthouses, and more than a dozen impossibly charming seaside towns. It's an ideal spot to both relax and recharge.

Many visitors to the Cape return to the same town year after year, rarely venturing beyond their favorite beach, ice cream stand, and seafood shack. The best Cape Cod travel advice is that you may need more than one trip to explore it all.

You haven't reached the Cape until you have crossed the Cape Cod Canal, the narrow channel of water that separates the Cape from the rest of Massachusetts. You'll rattle over either the Sagamore or Bourne Bridge, spotting boats in the water and the sandy, pine-dotted landscape beyond. When you roll down the window to inhale the briny air—that's when you know you have arrived.

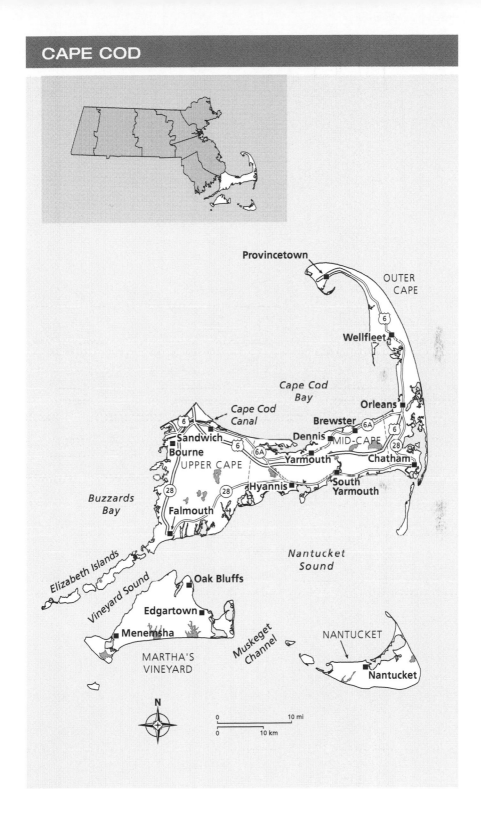

AUTHOR'S TOP TEN PICKS

Art's Dune Tours
4 Standish St.
Provincetown
(508) 487-1950
artsdunetours.com

Capeabilities Farm
458 Main St.
Dennis
(508) 385-2538
capeabilitiesfarm.com

Cape Cod National Seashore
99 Marconi Site Rd.
Wellfleet
(508) 255-3421
nps.gov/caco

Cape Cod Rail Trail
3488 Main St.
Brewster
(508) 896-3491
mass.gov/locations/cape-cod-rail-trail

Chappaquiddick Island
Martha's Vineyard
chappyferry.com

Edward Gorey House
8 Strawberry Ln.
Yarmouth Port
(508) 362-3909
edwardgoreyhouse.org

Nantucket Shipwreck & Lifesaving Museum
158 Polpis Rd.
Nantucket
(508) 228-1885
eganmaritime.org

Nickerson State Park
3488 Main St.
Brewster
(508) 896-3491
mass.gov/locations/nickerson-state-park

The Sandwich Glass Museum
129 Main St.
Sandwich
(508) 888-0251
sandwichglassmuseum.org

The Woods Hole Oceanographic Institute
93 Water St.
Woods Hole
(508) 289-2252
whoi.edu

Bourne

All roads to Cape Cod lead to Bourne. It is really where Cape Cod begins. State Route 6A, known as the "Old King's Highway," starts here, stretching 34 miles as it meanders by fields, farms, and salt marshes and detours to sandy white beaches when you feel like stopping.

Your first stop over the Sagamore Bridge should be the town of Bourne and the *Apatuxet Trading Post Museum* (508-759-9487; bournehistorical society.org), which conveys a sense of the Cape's very long history. The reconstructed settlement dates from 1627. A small group of Pilgrims from Plimouth established the post for the three-way trade of salt, animal furs, and linen with the Wampanoags and the Dutch traders from New Amsterdam. The museum is part of the Bourne Historical Society's campus, located at 24 Apatuxet Road. Among other sites on the property is a little Bourne train station, built for the exclusive use of President Grover Cleveland for his journey from Washington, DC, to his Buzzards Bay summerhouse, Gray Gables. The museum is open Memorial Day weekend through mid-October, Thursday through Saturday, from 10 a.m. to 4 p.m. Admission is $6 for adults and $4 for children.

Sandwich

First settled in 1637, Sandwich is one of the quieter spots on the Cape, but it has a lot going on for a town of just twenty thousand residents. Its location close to the Sagamore Bridge has helped establish the town as a year-round community that supports a large number of restaurants and shops in its charming and historic downtown. The town also has several inns that are open year-round, making it an ideal base for an off-season (and budget-friendly) Cape visit.

Hidden in plain view within a residential neighborhood, the *Heritage Museum & Gardens* (508-888-3300; heritagemuseumsandgardens.org) is a true Cape Cod gem. The one-hundred-acre woodland is well known for its impressive collection of rhododendrons, azaleas, and hydrangeas, but there is beauty in bloom in all seasons here and miles of paved paths to explore it all. Spend some time viewing the museum's eclectic holdings of folk art and its collection of forty-two antique American motorcars, including an 1899 Winton carriage and a 1913 Ford Model T. Museum admission also includes a ride (or two, or three) on the hand-carved 1908 Looff carousel.

The museum is located at 87 Grove Street and is open late April through mid-October, daily from 10 a.m. to 5 p.m. Admission is $21 for adults, $11 for children.

trivia

After bartering, the use of wampum—beads made from quahog shells in a dizzying array of white, blue, and purple hues—was the go-to method of payment among the Native tribes of the East Coast. As early as the 1630s, the colonies at Jamestown, New Amsterdam, and Plimoth accepted wampum for trade with Native tribes as well as among one another to replace coinage, which was scarce in the colonies. Wampum is considered Massachusetts's first currency; it was recognized by the Massachusetts Bay Colony as legal tender in 1650 and was the de facto "coin of the realm" for the next thirty years.

TOP ANNUAL EVENTS

MARCH

Cape Cod St. Patrick's Day Parade
Yarmouth
(508) 240-7347
capecodstpatricksparade.com

APRIL

Nantucket Daffodil Festival
Nantucket
(508) 228-1700
nantucketchamber.org/daffodilfestival

JUNE

Nantucket Film Festival
Nantucket
(646) 480-1900
nantucketfilmfestival.org

JULY

Barnstable County Fair
East Falmouth
(508) 563-3200
capecodfairgrounds.com

Cape Cod Hydrangea Fest
Cape-wide
capecodhydrangeafest.com

Mashpee Wampanoag Powwow
Mashpee
(508) 477-0208
mashpeewampanoagtribe-nsn.gov

AUGUST

Falmouth Road Race
Falmouth
(508) 540-7000
falmouthroadrace.com

Martha's Vineyard Agricultural Fair
West Tisbury
(508) 693-9549
marthasvineyardagriculturalsociety.org

Provincetown Carnival
Provincetown
(508) 487-2313
ptown.org/carnival

Woods Hole Film Festival
Woods Hole
(508) 495-3456
woodsholefilmfestival.org

OCTOBER

Wellfleet Oyster Fest
Wellfleet
(508) 349-3499
wellfleetspat.org

Yarmouth Seaside Festival
South Yarmouth
yarmouthseasidefestival.com

DECEMBER

Christmas Stroll
Nantucket
(508) 228-1700
nantucketchamber.org/stroll

Holidays by the Sea
Falmouth
(508) 548-8500
falmouthchamber.com

Sandwich is a fine walking village. The historic **Dexter Grist Mill** and the seventeenth-century **Hoxie House** (508-888-1173; sandwichmass.org) provide a glimpse into colonial times and are located within walking distance of each other on extremely picturesque Shawme Pond. The Hoxie House is a restored 1675 saltbox colonial and is considered the oldest home on the Cape.

The primitive house has just three rooms—two on the first floor and a large sleeping chamber up the ladderlike stairs on the second floor. Among the highlights are the cooking implements and a weaving loom; all the artifacts are originals, and some are on loan from the Boston Museum of Fine Arts. The water-powered Dexter Grist Mill dates from 1637; grinding corn and wheat into flour was considered an essential service in colonial times. This is a working mill, with extremely knowledgeable docents telling the story of seventeenth-century technological processes and working the mill at the same time. More than three tons of corn are milled annually, and the cornmeal is available for purchase. Cornmeal from a working 1600s grist mill is a pretty nifty souvenir. Hoxie House is at 18 Water Street; Dexter Grist Mill is at the corner of Water and Grove Streets. The properties are open seasonally from June through October; check the website for days and times. Admission is $5 adults and $3 for children.

In the heart of Sandwich Village at 1 Water Street, **The Dunbar House Tea Room** (508-833-2485; thedunbarhouse.com) has been delighting visitors for decades with finger sandwiches (smoked salmon, cucumber, and deviled egg), freshly baked scones, bite-size cakes, and an extensive tea list. Mood. Note: They also have a light lunch menu.

From the Dexter Grist Mill, it is a short five-minute walk to the **Sandwich Glass Museum** (508-888-0251; sandwichglassmuseum.org). Back in the day, Sandwich was the center of pressed-glass making in America. In 1825 Deming Jarves of Boston established the Boston and Sandwich Glass company in Sandwich, initially specializing in blown-glass decorative objects, including whale-oil lamps and jugs. By the mid-1800s, glassmaking technology had improved to utilize a lever-operated pressing machine, and the company became renowned for its lacy opalescent molded-glass tableware in hues of blue, purple, green, yellow, and red. Special exhibits feature the work of contemporary glass artists and help keep the museum fresh. Be sure to time your visit to take in a narrated glassblowing demonstration, offered every hour on the hour. The gift shop is better than average, with items that range from suncatchers and Christmas ornaments to museum-quality sculptures. The museum is located at 129 Main Street and is open daily April through December from 10 a.m. to 5 p.m. The museum is closed for the month of January and open again in February and March, Wednesday through Sunday, from 9:30 a.m. to 4 p.m. Admission is $12 for adults and $2 for children.

Just down a country lane along the Old King's Highway at 6 Discovery Hill Road, you will find the **Thornton W. Burgess Society/Green Briar Nature Center & Jam Kitchen** (508-888-6870; thorntonburgess.org). It is an enchanting spot that inspired beloved Sandwich children's author Thornton Burgess's magical tales of Peter Rabbit, Jimmy Skunk, Reddy Fox, and other friends. The Briar Patch conservation area comprises fifty-seven acres and has a nature trail by a clear kettle pond and through white cedar swamps and fields. Gardeners will want to take a stroll through the Shirley Cross Wildflower Garden. For a taste of old Cape Cod, check out the 1900-era jam kitchen and gift shop. Better yet, sign up for a jam-making class using the kitchen's tried-and-true recipes. The beach plum jelly bursts with memories of summer and is the shop's best-seller. Suggested donation is $5 for adults and $3 for children. Jam-making classes are additional and must be reserved in advance. The property is open Tuesday through Saturday from 10 a.m. to 3 p.m.

Falmouth

On the southwestern edge of Cape Cod, Falmouth is just thirteen miles from the Bourne Bridge—making this one of the closest Cape destinations to Boston. If you want to mix a summer beach vacation with a village feel, look no further. The town green, a colonial militia training ground during the Revolutionary War, is surrounded by stately Federal and Georgian homes and a Main Street with lots of shops.

Head south toward Vineyard Sound and you'll come across a small harbor village of salt-aged clapboard houses and wood wharves. Most visitors come to Woods Hole to board a ferry for Martha's Vineyard, but look just beyond the docks and you'll see the telltale blocky buildings of an academic community. What was once a fishing station has evolved to become the home of the Woods Hole Oceanographic Institute (WHOI), renowned as an international center for marine, biomedical, and environmental research.

Curious minds of all ages can geek out at the **Woods Hole Oceano-graphic Institute** (508-289-2252; whoi.edu). Guided walking tours along the docks give visitors a glimpse inside the work of the institute; including seeing the research vessels and small robots that are being used for WHOI's current research projects. Inside, at the Discovery Center, there are interactive exhibits for kids as well as an exhibit on *Alvin*, the submersible vessel that led to the 1985 discovery of the *Titanic*. The main takeaway: Science is awesome. Your first stop should be the visitor center at 93 Water Street, open Monday through Saturday from 11 a.m. to 5 p.m., to see what's on for the day. Check the website in advance of your visit. The institute's lectures are excellent—and some are open to the public.

A favorite of town residents and locals in the know, **Wood Neck Beach** (508-548-8623; falmouthma.gov) is a super low-key stretch of sand that features sea vistas on one side and tidal river views of Little Sippewissett Marsh on the other. This is an ideal, quiet beach for little ones, with horseshoe crabs in the sandbars and dune grasses for exploring. It's also a great choice for parents who want to read a book while gentle waves tickle their toes.

Beach fees are collected from mid-June through Labor Day through a parking fee, and this beach parking lot is for residents only. But walk-ons to the beach (or cyclists or drop-offs) don't even need a sticker. To find the beach, head out of town along curvy Sippewissett Road to 33 Woodneck Beach Road.

Need a beach break? ***Spohr Gardens*** (508-548-0623; spohrgardens .com), overlooking Oyster Pond, was once the home of Falmouth residents Charles and Margaret Spohr, who donated the property for the enjoyment of the public. Starting with a sea of daffodils in April, the pathways of this six-acre garden that blooms with perennials from summer through fall. There's a wonderful collection of trees as well (the beeches are a standout). Charles Spohr was an avid collector of both antique anchors and millstones—be on the lookout for several pieces from his collection used as sculptural garden art. The garden is located 45 Fells Road and is open daily from 8 a.m. to 8 p.m. Admission is free.

Hyannis

Hyannis is a village (and a very large one at that) of the larger town of Barnstable. John F. Kennedy put Hyannis on the map when he stayed at the Kennedy Compound, the family's summer home, during his time as president.

Hyannis serves as the portal to the Cape; trains, buses, and planes from Boston and afar connect here, as do ferries to Martha's Vineyard and Nantucket. The Cape's only hospital, Cape Cod Hospital, and the region's only mall, the Cape Cod Mall, are here too. There is always a lot going on here.

When the weather and ferry schedule favor strolling, it's a pleasant walk along the water. Hyannis is homeport to vessels that range from small runabouts to mega yachts, making boat watching a choice activity.

Just off Main Street, at 135 South Street, the ***Cape Cod Maritime Museum*** (508-775-1723; capecodmaritimemuseum.org) is a little gem of a museum that's jam-packed with all things related to Cape Cod's more than four hundred years of seafaring heritage. Find exhibits on the Pilgrims, whaling in Provincetown, and the history of shellfishing in the region. Don't miss visiting the boatyard to watch volunteers restore and build boats, and pop into the historic barn to see a diverse collection of Cape wooden boats. For an unforgettable excursion, book a 90-minute cruise of Hyannis Harbor on the museum's 1886 replica catboat, *Sarah*. It's an intimate cruise; the boat accommodates just six passengers, and tickets are a bargain at $45. The museum is open Wednesday through Saturday from 10 a.m. to 4 p.m. Admission is $10 for adults and $8 for children ages six through seventeen.

Ice cream lovers have dozens of choices on the Cape. ***Four Seas Ice Cream*** (508-775-1394; fourseasicecream.com) has the distinction of being the Cape's oldest ice cream shop, having opened its doors in 1934. The ice cream is made on-site, and there are twenty-plus flavors available at any given time, but New England traditional flavors like penuche and fresh strawberry very much rule. Look for this landmark shop at 360 South Main Street in the Barnstable village of Centreville.

Yarmouth

Yarmouth has traditionally been one of the Cape's more family-focused towns, with an emphasis on the simple joys of summer—a day at the beach, a round of miniature golf, and ice cream every night.

The ***Edward Gorey House*** (508-362-3909; edwardgoreyhouse.org) is dedicated to celebrating the work of the enigmatic illustrator and author who is perhaps best known as the animator of the opening sequence of the PBS show *Mystery!* Gorey bought a sea captain's home in 1979 and lived and worked here until his death in 2000. The house remains largely as he left it—chock-full of his many collections, including books, cheese graters, and Beanie Babies. A highlight for many is the collection of original sketches for *The Gashleycrumb Tinies*, a very Gorey (as in dark and quirky) alphabet book that tells of the untimely demise of twenty-six unfortunate children: "A is for Amy who fell down the stairs, B is for Basil assaulted by bears." Dracula and felines are prominent throughout the house as well—Gorey won a Tony award for his costume designs for the Broadway production of *Dracula*. He was also an ardent animal rights activist. The house is at 8 Strawberry Lane and is open mid-April through December; check the website for days and times. Admission is $8 for adults and $2 for children.

Dennis

Dennis is firmly the halfway point of the Cape. The town spans the width of the peninsula, offering two distinctive beach experiences: placid Cape Cod Bay and the wavier Nantucket Sound.

Is that the beach calling? While throngs of beachgoers compete for space at Mayflower Beach, you can relax at ***Chapin Memorial Beach*** (508-760-6159; town.dennis.ma.us/beach-department), a smaller and quiet patch of sand with top-notch views of Sandy Neck Light. The beach is at 90 Chapin Beach Road; parking is $30 a day (cash only).

Movies are the ultimate rainy day Cape Cod activity. For nearly one hundred years, the nostalgic *Cape Cinema* (508-385-2503; capecinema.com) has attracted filmgoers for its mix of blockbusters, art films, indie favorites, and timeless classics. It's a legendary venue; the world premiere of *The Wizard of Oz* took place here on August 11, 1939. Margaret Hamilton, the Wicked Witch of the West, was performing at the next-door Cape Playhouse and made it happen. It's a special setting for cinephiles, with an eye-catching Rockwell Kent Art Deco ceiling mural that features stylized nude figures and an abstract, impressionist view of the heavens. The theater is located at 35 Hope Lane and is an integral part of the year-round Cape Cod community.

Very much off the beaten path, deep amid the pines on bucolic Scargo Lake, *Scargo Pottery* (508-385-3894; scargopottery.com) has been a shopping destination for visitors to the Cape since the 1950s. Located at 30 Doctor Lord's Road, the indoor/outdoor artisan-run gallery space offers whimsical garden pieces, lamp bases, and durable, unpretentious handmade pieces to set the table every day. The Scargo coffee mug is a visitor favorite.

An observation tower on Scargo Hill has welcomed visitors to Dennis since 1874. The first of three towers was built by a prominent local family to drum up business for their next-door hotel, the Nobscussett. The original wood tower was downed by a gale in 1876, it was rebuilt, only to be destroyed by a fire in 1900. Very much a Three Little Pigs building situation, the final version of the tower is the present one, built with cobblestone in 1901. It's just thirty-eight steps to the top of the circular tower, which offers commanding views of the entire Cape—on a clear day you can see as far as Provincetown. The address for *Scargo Tower* is simply Scargo Hill Road. The site is maintained by the Town of Dennis; hours are 6 a.m. to 10 p.m., and admission is free.

Cruising the Cape Cod Rail Trail

This twenty-five-mile continuous band of asphalt begins in Yarmouth and winds through Dennis, Harwich, Brewster, Orleans, and Eastham, offering postcard-perfect views of forest, kettle ponds, horse farms, and cranberry bogs as you zip along on two wheels. The route roughly runs parallel to Old King's Highway (State Route 6A), and there are eleven bike shops directly on the path as well as numerous restaurants and ice cream shops where you can recharge along the way. *Cape Cod Rail Trail* (508-896-3491; mass.gov/locations/cape-cod-rail-trail).

It's not far from Scargo Tower to 458 Main Street and the market stand for **Capeabilities Farm** (508-385-2538; capeabilitiesfarm.com), which provides employment and a welcoming community to people with developmental and intellectual disabilities. The farm began as a modest tomato greenhouse employing three workers in 2006 and has grown to an operation that employs more than eighty people of all abilities in the greenhouses, market, and an eight-acre farm in nearby Marstons Mills. In addition to their own fresh-picked produce, the stand stocks cheese, bread, chip, deli meats, pasta, and sauce—in short, everything you need to stock your weekly rental.

Brewster

The road is a winding one as you reach Brewster—unique among Cape Cod towns, as all its beaches are on Cape Cod Bay, where the water is calmer, warmer, and usually seaweed free. Brewster's Main Street is dotted with eighteenth- and nineteenth-century sea captains' homes; many have been converted into boutique hotels or charming restaurants.

Brewster has some of the most formidable tides in America. The **Brewster Flats** are considered the largest flats in North America and extend nearly ten miles along the Brewster coast to North Eastham. At low tide you can walk nearly two miles out along Brewster's tidal flats, making this a perfect spot for sunsets, sandcastles, or getting your step count up. You can also see active oyster farms. Popular spots to access the flats are Breakwater, Paine's Creek, Ellis Landing, and Linnell Landing Roads. Be sure to check the tide charts to help you time your visit.

You'll find pine needles mixed with sand at **Nickerson State Park** (508-896-3491; mass.gov/locations/nickerson-state-park), located directly on the eleven-mile mark of the Cape Cod Rail Trail. Nickerson boasts miles of hiking and biking trails for exploring, as well as eight crystal-clear kettle ponds that were formed by retreating ice age glaciers. If it's a hot day, don't hesitate to jump in—the water is the perfect temperature for floating. The 1,900-acre park's parking lot address is 3488 Main Street. Nickerson has long been a popular choice for camping, with four hundred campsites as well as a handful of yurts (book well in advance). Park day-use fees are $8 for Massachusetts residents, $30 for nonresidents.

The favorite Cape Cod Rail Trail pit stop in these parts is **Cobie's** (508-896-7021; cobies.com) at 3260 Main Street (also down the road from Nickerson). Roadside to the trail, Cobie's has been in business since 1948 and specializes in fried clams, seafood, burgers, hot dogs, and ice cream—it's pretty much a restaurant designed for summer on the Cape.

What is better than getting lost in the world of books? The ***Brewster Book Store*** (508-896-6543; brewsterbookstore.com) has been at 2648 Main Street since 1982 and is a great place to putter, and inevitably buy, as it has something for all tastes. Open year-round, the store has quite a reputation for hosting regular literary events, including author talks, signings, and story times for kids.

Chatham

Chatham, positioned at the "elbow" of the Cape, is posh but unpretentious, with a Main Street of charming boutiques and excellent restaurants. It's the kind of place where the town's band plays big band classics in the park on summer Friday nights—and more than a few couples get up to sway cheek to cheek.

Rock Harbor (Rock Harbor Road, Chatham) is one of the most magical places on Cape Cod. The quaint, working fishing harbor faces west over Cape Cod Bay and offers one of the most mind-blowing sunsets the Cape has to offer. On your way, pull off into the parking lot near the docks and walk over to ***Young's Seafood Shack*** (508-255-3366; nausetfishandlobsterpool.com/youngs-fish-market) at 113 Rock Harbor Road for a lobster roll and a bowl of clam chowder to take to the beach. When the sun dips into the bay, the crowd claps, and boats honk. It's dinner and a show for cheap.

The best—and some may say the only—way to rent a kayak on Cape Cod is from a place right on the water. ***Chatham Kayak*** (508-241-5389; chatham kayak.com) is located on Oyster Pond, an ideal place for even first-timers. Although motorboats share these waters, they stick to a five-mile-per-hour speed limit and will give you wide berth. For an even more unique view of

Take Me Out to a Cape Cod Baseball League Game

Nearly every summer evening, just as twilight descends, stadium lights illuminate the small-town fields where the ten teams of the *Cape Cod Baseball League* (capecod baseball.org) play ball. Seated on picnic blankets and beach chairs, fans come in droves to see the nation's most talented college baseball players get their start—you might just see the next Chris Sale.

Between innings, parents play catch with their kids, or there might be a raffle sale or a T-shirt toss. It's a forty-game season, and Cape Cod League teams play nearly every summer day. The team towns are Bourne, Brewster, Chatham, Cotuit, Falmouth, Harwich, Hyannis, Orleans, Wareham, and Yarmouth-Dennis, so it is easy to find a game nearby. Games are free, but donations are accepted.

Cape Cod from the water, rent a stand-up paddleboard. The docks are easy to find at 391 Barn Hill Road, just off Main Street.

A long paddle deserves a reward, and **Mom and Pops Burgers** (774-840-4144; momandpopschatham.com) doesn't disappoint. It's conveniently located at 1603 Main Street at the intersection of Barn Hill Road on the way back from Chatham Kayak and Harding's Beach. Mom is from the Philippines; Dad is from New England. Together, their version of the great American classic is particularly winning. All is accompanied by first-rate fries. And did we mention the beer flights?

Orleans

On to Orleans, one of the smallest towns on the Cape. Stop at Town Cove Park (intersection of State Routes 28 and 6A) a pretty, green space for picnicking or just stretching your legs. The 1720 **Johnathan Young Windmill** is a stop-in kind of place during July and August, when it is staffed by volunteers, and is also a prime picture-taking spot.

The **French Cable Station Museum** (508-240-1735; frenchcablestation museum.org) at 41 South Orleans Road is a fascinating little place that charts the unlikely tale of Orleans's role in early transatlantic communications. In 1898, a 3,200-mile underwater cable, "Le Direct," was laid here from Brest, France, and was used for the transmission of telegraphic messages from Europe until 1959. The devoted museum volunteers take tremendous pride in explaining the telegraph station's history and demonstrate the still-functioning vintage equipment. It takes just about an hour to see all the exhibits, and admission is free—making this a great choice to break up a day at the beach. The museum is open June through September, Friday through Sunday, from 1 to 4 p.m.

Tucked into a cove, **South Orleans Beach** on Pleasant Bay is the town's secret beach. There are no frills (read: no amenities) here, but there are far fewer people than either at Nauset or Skaket, the surf is gentle, and it's free. The landing divides the beach; one side is public, the other is private. There is no parking lot, it is street parking only.

Wellfleet

Surrounded by the coast on two sides, Wellfleet has a long history of harboring whalers and fishermen. Wellfleet is much less developed than its neighbors, tony Chatham and raucous Provincetown. Today, Wellfleet's rustic beauty and remoteness draw artistic and literary types who seek refuge in its quiet, natural environment.

The town's annual Oyster Fest is a notable exception, bringing thousands of visitors to town over one October weekend to enjoy crate upon crate of Wellfleet's world-renowned bivalves, washed down with classic New England beer.

Visit Wellfleet until dark, and then catch a flick at the wonderfully retro **Wellfleet Drive-In** (508-348-2450; wellfleetcinemas.com), one of the last of its kind in Massachusetts. Order tickets online in advance (general admission is $15 per person), come early to choose the best parking spot, and then tune your radio to the soundtrack to enjoy the double feature of first-run, family-friendly films under the stars. There is a concession stand for intermission snack runs—or you can bring your own. The season runs from May through Labor Day weekend. The Wellfleet Drive-In is located on US 6 at the Wellfleet and Eastham town line.

Upgrade your day at the sea with a visit to a true secret Cape Cod beach. **Bound Brook Island Beach** is part of the Cape Cod National Seashore, but with any luck you can make it all your own. Accessing the beach requires a one-mile trek down unpaved Coles Neck Road. Park at the Atwood Higgins House, the National Park Service property at 269 Bound Brook Island Road, and take a minimalist approach to the gear you bring. Be on the lookout for the sandy path through the towering dunes and beach grass; walk another quarter mile and you'll be treated to pure, isolated bliss—a place to ponder, with unbeatable vistas of unspoiled white sand and glittering water.

Start your adventure at the **Wellfleet Bay Wildlife Sanctuary** (508-349-2615; massaudubon.org) with a stop by the Nature Center, a bit of an underappreciated gem that is part outdoor exploration, part indoor learning center, and all very uniquely Cape Cod. There are five miles of family-friendly trails at this Massachusetts Audubon property. With mudflats, salt marsh, pitch pine woods, and a big finish across the raised boardwalk to the beach, you can knock out all kinds of landscapes in one fell swoop. If you are interested in nature photography, come early in the day to make use of the bird blinds. The visitor center address is 291 US 6; it is open daily late May through mid-September, 9 a.m. to 4 p.m. The trails are open year-round from dawn to dusk. Admission is $8 for adults and $3 for children.

Provincetown

No one ever comes to Provincetown by accident. Located at the very tip of Cape Cod, when you are here, it seems as though you are at the end of the world. It is a beach town of unparalleled wild, natural beauty that, together with its remoteness, has always drawn outsiders: whalers, pirates, artists, and writers.

Few small towns are as multilayered as Provincetown. The area has a long fishing heritage; the Wampanoag and Nauset people knew these waters well. As early as the 1400s, intrepid fishing boats from European countries likely fished these grounds for cod—well before the Pilgrims arrived on these sandy shores. Fishermen from the Azores arrived in Provincetown in the mid-1800s. To this day, much of the population is of Portuguese heritage.

P-town, as it is affectionately known, has always been a welcoming place, and it has been an enduring summer destination for the gay community for nearly a century. Provincetown's walkable, historic downtown streets are lined with LGBTQ+–friendly restaurants, art galleries, and a vibrant nightlife scene.

Be forewarned: The town's year-round residents number three thousand, but during the summer, Provincetown is positively heaving with a population that swells to more than sixty thousand. And since the only way to drive into town is along US 6, the summer traffic can be epic.

The Provincetown Dunes are part of the Cape Cod National Seashore. It's an otherworldly landscape of windblown sand, crashing waves, and incredible light. The dunes were formed when the earliest settlers cut down the trees that held the sand in place. The dunes have long attracted artists and writers. In the early 1900s, several US Life-Saving Service huts were converted to artist shacks, the solitude attracting artists Eugene O'Neill, Jackson Pollock, and Tennessee Williams, who were all inspired to work and create here. Access to the dunes is strictly controlled by the National Park Service. You can walk in via US 6 (park on the northbound side). It's a challenging, unprotected one-mile hike across the sand, so be sure to bring water and sunscreen. The other option is to be driven in by *Art's Dune Tours* (508-487-1950; artsdunetours.com), which has been ferrying visitors to the dunes for more than seventy-five years. The Art's Dune Tours meeting point is at 4 Standish Street. Tours are by SUV and take place daily April through November. The popular one-hour tour is offered several times a day and costs $38 per person. Sunset tours are offered as well.

Before or after the beach, a stop by *The Canteen* (508-487-3800; thecan teenptown.com) at 225 Commercial Street is in order. It is the local go-to fish shack for lobster rolls, fish-and-chips, and frosé with a view.

Up for a challenge? The *Provincetown Causeway Hike* is for you. The two-and-a-half-mile out-and-back trail is not for the faint of heart—you'll be walking across tumbled granite boulders piled high and strung across the Provincetown Harbor. But the payoff is huge—you can see two lighthouses on this trip, Wood End and Long Point, and enjoy a phenomenal panoramic view of Provincetown. Look for the trailhead at Province Lands Road near Pilgrims First Landing Park. Note that it takes a good hour to walk across the dike and another hour to return. Give yourself more time if you want to spend time at the lighthouses—and be sure to check the tide times, or you may be stranded. Note: Neither Wood End nor Long Point is open for tours.

The **Shark Center Provincetown** (508-348-5901; atlanticwhiteshark.org) at 16 MacMillan Pier is an off-the-beaten-path attraction simply because it is brand-new and not well known—at least not yet. Opened in May 2022, the museum is the second outpost of the Atlantic White Shark Conservancy (the other is in Chatham). The Cape is a hotbed of great white shark activity because sharks are attracted to the region's large population of seals. The museum has created an immersive underwater-like experience using lights, sound, and imagery to support its mission to engage and educate the public to demystify white sharks while promoting ocean conservation efforts. The museum is totally appropriate for families and offers a meaningful way to connect with science and ongoing local shark research. The center is open daily from Memorial Day weekend through October, 10 a.m. to 4 p.m. Admission is $12.

trivia

The Pilgrims first landed in Provincetown, not Plymouth. The storm-battled *Mayflower* arrived in Provincetown Harbor on November 11, 1620. The Pilgrims then spent five weeks exploring the area, looking for a freshwater source and more arable land than the tip of Cape Cod offered. They ultimately sailed across Cape Cod Bay to settle in the area known as Patuxet by the Wampanoag, which the Pilgrims named New Plimoth. It was while the Pilgrims were anchored at Provincetown that they signed the Mayflower Compact, which established rules of self-government, setting an early precedent for independence in the new colony.

Martha's Vineyard

Martha's Vineyard, or simply "the Vineyard," is just six miles out to sea, but when you step off the ferry, the regular world just seems to disappear.

Offering captivating views, windswept beaches, and ample opportunities for outdoor exploits of every kind, Martha's Vineyard is also home to six authentically charming towns. The "Down-Island" town are the port towns: Edgartown's elegant captain's homes are linked to the prosperity of the island's whaling port days; Oak Bluffs draws hordes of visitors to its neighborhood of nineteenth-century gingerbread cottages; and Vineyard Haven, also known as Tisbury, is known as the island's commercial center. "Up-Island" are the towns on the western half of the island: rustic-chic West Tisbury; Chilmark, along with its fishing village of Menemsha; and Aquinnah, ancestral home of the island's Wampanoag and famed for its jaw-dropping clay cliffs.

Getting to Martha's Vineyard

Martha's Vineyard is an island; there are no tunnels or bridges connecting it to main-land Massachusetts. Most visitors will need to fly or take a ferry—but the journey is well worth it.

The **Steamship Authority** (steamshipauthority.com) is the quasi-governmental agency that provides year-round ferry service for passengers and vehicles from Woods Hole. You can walk on any of the Steamship Authority's crossings, but you must make a reservation in advance if you are bringing your car.

The Steamship Authority has by far the most crossings of all the operators—as many as twelve departures daily in the high season. During summer additional passenger-only ferries leave from Hyannis (Hyline Cruises; hylinecruises.com), Falmouth (Island Queen; islandqueen.com), and New Bedford (Seastreak Ferries; seastreak.com).

There are no ferries from Boston to Martha's Vineyard!

It's Friday. You have just arrived on the Vineyard Haven ferry, and you are famished. It is just a five-minute walk up Main Street to *Grace Episcopal Church* (508-693-0332; graceepiscopalmv.org), which offers some of the best lobster rolls in town. Grace Church lobster rolls, a delicious island tradition, are served at 34 Woodlawn Street from mid-May through Labor Day, 4 p.m. to 7 p.m. The lobster rolls, clam chowder, hot dogs, and pie are very well priced. It's a weekly bonding event for the island—and the public is welcome.

Take a walk in Oak Bluffs in the evening after dinner, and you might not notice the sneakily hidden *Back Door Doughnuts* (508-693-3699; backdoor donuts.com) except for the deep-fried aroma of cinnamon and sugar, making you think that you *need* a doughnut now. Follow your nose and find the line queuing in the alleyway behind 1-11 Kennebec Avenue. The must-order is the old-fashioned apple fritter—fresh from the oven and melt-in-your-mouth deli-cious. The "back-door" season is from Memorial Day weekend to mid-October, 7 p.m. to midnight. (The front-of-the shop is open year-round.)

Set out from Down Island to Up Island with a drive to the westernmost tip of the Vineyard. The sparkling Atlantic Ocean from atop the red clay cliffs of Aquinnah is a museum-worthy sight. Aquinnah means "land under the hill." Wampanoag legend says that the giant Moshup provided food for his people by flinging whales against the towering cliffs, staining the rocks red. The cliffs are sacred to the tribe and are protected territory.

On the way to or from Aquinnah, you may stumble upon *Orange Peel Bakery* (508-645-2025; orangepeelbakery.net) on the side of the road. Founded by Juli Vanderhoop, this Native-owned micro-artisan bakery is a community gathering place on sacred Wampanoag land. There are glossy cinnamon snails and buttery broccoli and Gouda quiches. Crunchy, chewy sourdough and salted caramel cookies wrapped and ready to go to the beach are all baked on the premises in the outdoor wood-fired clay oven. On Thursday evenings from April through November, Vanderhoop's famed pizza nights are the place to be. During summer there are wood-oven Sunday dinners, like codfish and sausage with littleneck clams along with corn fritters and spicy aioli. Open year-round, the address is 22 State Road. In the off-season, the bakery has an honor payment system, so bring cash.

If it is open, pull over along the way to view the *Aquinnah Lighthouse* (508-645-2300; gayheadlight.org). There has been a lighthouse on this spot since 1799; this version dates from the 1850s. The lighthouse is sometimes referred to as Gay Head Light, as that was the English name for the area until the town voted to reinstate its original Native name in 1998. The lighthouse is at the end of Lighthouse Road and is open beginning in June, Friday through Monday from 10 a.m. to 4 p.m. In July and August it is open daily from 10 a.m. to 4 p.m. and September through mid-October Friday through Monday from 10 a.m. to 4 p.m. Admission is $6 for adults and free for children age twelve and under.

Trade packed beaches for the peace and quiet of the relatively untouched shoreline of *Great Rock Bight Preserve* (mvlandbank.com) in Chilmark. To find the trailhead, look for the Chilmark fire station on North Street and drive a half mile down single-lane Brickyard Road to a small parking lot. From here you will need to bushwhack down the bluff to the sandy, secluded cove. It's a picture-perfect stretch of sand with great surf and lots of room to spread out.

Pack a picnic and visit at sunset. Great Rock Bight is west facing, and the show is just as good as at nearby Menemsha—minus the crowds.

Polly Hill Arboretum (508-693-9426; pollyhillarboretum.org) is living proof that the New England coast can be a great place to garden despite the salt air and wind. The garden is the legacy of Polly Hill, who in 1958 took over her family's summer place at the age of fifty and began planting. The setting is mostly woodland and meadow; highlights include the perennial border, the dogwood allée, and the monkey puzzle tree. The seventy-acre public garden is located at 795 State Road in West Tisbury. It is open from mid-May through mid-October; hours are 9:30 a.m. to 4:30 p.m. Admission is $5 for adults and free for children age twelve and under.

The Vineyard is home to many interesting small galleries, most of which display works of local artists or art that is inspired by the island. On the way to Aquinnah, the *Field Gallery Sculpture Garden* (508-693-5595; fieldgallery .com) features whimsical white female sculptures frolicking on a lawn. The figures are the work of founder Tom Maley and date from 1971. Strike a pose and take a photo—everyone does. As you drive along State Road, the larger-than-life sculptures on the grounds of the Field Gallery at 1050 State Road are difficult to miss. Gallery hours are Monday through Saturday from 10 a.m. to 5 p.m., Sunday 11 a.m. to 4 p.m.

A public Vineyard beach that is often overlooked by visitors, *Lighthouse Beach* at 230 North Water Street is just a half-mile walk from tony Edgartown's main drag. There is no lifeguard on duty, but the surf is generally mellow; and if you stop by *Among the Flowers* (508-627-3233; amongtheflowersmv.com) at 17 Mayhew Lane for sandwiches beforehand, you won't miss the concession stand.

A visit to the Vineyard isn't complete without visiting at least one of the island's five lighthouses. *Edgartown Harbor Light* (508-627-4441; mvmuseum.org) is a favorite for its picturesque setting. This cast-iron beauty dates from 1875, but like a lot of Vineyarders, she is a wash-ashore, having come to the Vineyard from Ipswich to replace an earlier lighthouse that had been damaged in the New England Hurricane of 1938. Visitors can climb the spiral staircase to the top for views of Edgartown Harbor and Chappaquiddick Island. The lighthouse is located on Lighthouse Beach at 121 North Water Street and is open daily July through early September, 10 a.m. to 4 p.m. Admission is $5.

Plan an island escape from your island escape. *Chappaquiddick* is just off the Vineyard coast and is considered part of Edgartown. It can only be reached by taking your car or bike on a four-minute ferry ride across the harbor. Although just six square miles, "Chappy," as the locals call it, offers jaw-dropping natural beauty and plenty of space to roam.

trivia

The twin ferries that chug back and forth between Edgartown and Chappaquiddick, *On Time I* and *On Time II,* have no set schedule. The ferries run continuously from 6:30 a.m. to midnight, and so are always "on time."

There is a small year-round population of just over one hundred residents (and no shops or restaurants, so plan accordingly). Most of the island is conservation land owned and managed by the Trustees of Reservations.

Tip: Leave your car behind. The *Chappaquiddick Ferry* (chappyferry.com) takes only three cars at a time, and the wait can be hours in summer. Ferry fares are $4 per passenger, $6 for passenger and bike, $13 for car and driver. Before crossing over on the ferry, head over to *Martha's Vineyard Bike Rentals* (800-627-2763; marthasvinyardbike.com) at 1 Main Street to pick up bikes—visiting Chappy is a perfect half-day activity for even the casual, recreational cyclist.

It's an easy two-and-a-half-mile ride along a dirt road to your first destination, **Mitoi** (508-627-7689; thetrustees.org/place/mytoi), pronounced "my-toy," a Japanese-style wooded botanical garden featuring native and non-native flowers and plants, a bamboo grove, and a darling footbridge across a reflecting pool. It is a lovely place for pondering. The gardens are located at 41 Dike Road and are open May 30 through October 15, 9 a.m. to 5 p.m.; admission is $5 per person.

Just beyond the garden is Dike Bridge, where Ted Kennedy crashed his car into the water in 1969, resulting in the death of his passenger, Mary Jo Kopechne. Nearby is **East Beach**, also known as Leland Beach, a half-mile stretch of prime Atlantic beachfront; it's a wonderful spot to take a dip and cool off.

Ditch civilization altogether at **Cape Poge Wildlife Refuge** (508-627-3599; thetrustees.org/place/cape-poge-wildlife-refuge). Located on the eastern shore of the island at 40 Road to the Gut, this is Chappy's wild side and serves as an ecological preserve. It's a birders' paradise, with lesser-seen birds and miles of hiking and walking trails

Nantucket

Nantucket is a little triangular island that lies far out to sea. Nearly thirty miles off the coast of Cape Cod, it has always felt like a very special escape. It's a place of winding cobblestone lanes, shingled cottages, hydrangeas, and pristine beaches.

From the mid-1700s to the 1830s, whaling was Nantucket's lifeblood. Nantucket was the setting for Herman Melville's *Moby-Dick*, and the island still retains many of the landmarks and much of the character that sparked Melville's imagination.

Nantucket is a dreamy island getaway year-round. Part of its dreamlike quality is the ever-present fog—Nantucket is called the "Grey Lady" for a reason!

Yes, it is true that Nantucket is known for its exclusivity, and in summer it is a sophisticated, cosmopolitan destination that very much caters to the global elite. To come in winter is to experience the island differently; it's a slower pace and very much a down-home, small-town vibe.

Nantucket is the name of the island and of its one town. More than 40 percent of Nantucket is conservation land, so there is plenty to explore. Strolling the bluffs, kayaking Nantucket Harbor, and pedaling the bike paths that crisscross the island are just a few of the ways to enjoy its natural beauty.

Nantucket is a place where all roads lead to the beach, with all the sand and surf you could ask for. **Steps Beach**, on the north side of the island and

Getting to Nantucket

There is always a stream of ferries coming in and out of Nantucket Harbor. Most visitors will arrive by ferry from Hyannis. Both the **Steamship Authority** (steamship-authority.com) and Hy-Line Cruises (hylinecruises.com) operate year-round, offering one-hour "fast" ferry service from Hyannis. The Steamship Authority also offers traditional car and passenger ferries that make the trip in a little more than two hours—reservations for vehicles are required well in advance. There's also seasonal ferry service between Nantucket and New Bedford with **Seastreak Ferries** (seastreak .com).

walkable from town, is a slightly secret beach that is popular with locals. It's contiguous with Jetties Beach, but without the beachy bustle. Steps Beach has—as you might expect—steps that lead to a sandy cove and just-right surf. Also contributing to its under-the-radar status, there is limited parking, and there are no lifeguards. Access is off Cliff Road at Lincoln Avenue.

Whether you are looking for muffins and iced coffee before you hit the trails or a delightful picnic lunch of overstuffed sandwiches and lemonade to bring with you to the beach, you'll find it at **Something Natural** (508-228-0504; somethingnatural.com), which has been located at 50 Cliff Road for more than fifty years.

Born and raised in Nantucket, Maria Mitchell was America's first female astronomer. Largely self-taught, she was also the first woman elected to the American Academy of Arts and Sciences, paving the way for female scientists. Today, Mitchell is also lauded for her efforts to champion social reform, including the antislavery and suffrage movements. The **Maria Mitchell Association** (508-228-9198; mariamitchell.org) honors this most remarkable woman's life with a campus that includes an aquarium, observatory, and natural science museum. On summer Mondays and Wednesdays, join the astronomy team for "open nights" at Loines Observatory for guided views of the heavens through both the antique and state-of-the art telescopes. The campus is open during the summer Monday through Friday from 10 a.m. to 4 p.m., Saturday 10 a.m. to 1 p.m. Winter hours are Saturday from 10 a.m. to 2 p.m. Admission is $20 for adults and $12 for children and includes entrance to each museum and one Loines Observatory stargazing session (reservations required).

Shopping the *"Madaket Mall"* is perhaps the most non-touristy Nantucket activity of all. The Nantucket Recycling Center and Landfill (508-228-4262; nantucket-ma.gov), aka the dump, is considered one of the best shopping experiences on the island. The town manages a Take-It area that is separate from the Leave-It area. It is worth a look if you are biking the Madaket Bike Path. Tip: The best stuff of all is found in the fall after summerhouse clean-outs. The landfill's address is 186 Madaket Road; summer hours are Saturday and Sunday from 8 a.m. to 11:30 a.m., Wednesday through Friday from 8 a.m. to 2:30 p.m.

Those who like to hike but prefer the path less traveled will totally enjoy **Coskata-Coate Wildlife Refuge** (508-228-5646; thetrustees.org), one of the most pristine stretches of coastline on the Atlantic. A protected habitat for migrating shorebirds, there are sixteen miles of trails, including roads for over-sand four-wheel-drive vehicles. Check in at the gatehouse at Wauwinet Road before you head out. The Coskata Woods Trail hike is a favorite; it's a moderately challenging five-mile round-trip hike that does require a time commitment. The walk starts with a twisting path near some seriously impressive homes between the trail and the ocean then moves into the woods, where oak forest gives way to grassy dunes, and you pop out onto a deserted beach and a salt pond. Gatehouse hours are 9 a.m. to 5 p.m. Admission is free for pedestrians.

The **Nantucket Shipwreck & Lifesaving Museum** (508-228-1885; egan maritime.org) is located three miles out of town and on the edge of Folger's Marsh. Mariners used to refer to Nantucket as the "graveyard of the Atlantic." It's easy to spend a couple of hours at this terrific little museum, which showcases the history of Nantucket's shipwrecks, valiant rescues, infamous nor'easters, and more. The museum even has a free "Shipwreck Shuttle" that departs from the Nantucket Visitor Center (25 Federal Street) every hour on the half hour, starting at 9:30 a.m. The museum is at 158 Polpis Road and is open late May through October 10, Monday through Saturday from 10 a.m. to 5 p.m. Admission is $10 for adults, $5 for children.

trivia

"Gentle, Kind, True" are the words on an icon-style painting of a smiling Fred Rogers in one of his trademark cardigans at St. Paul's Episcopal Church (508-228-0916; stpaulschurchnantucket.org). Fred Rogers, the beloved host of *Mr. Rogers' Neighborhood*, summered in Nantucket at his Madaket home from the early 1960s until his passing in 2003. He was a summer parishioner of St. Paul's, and the painting is displayed on the wall next to his favorite pew. St. Paul's is an active congregation, but visitors are welcome to pop in to see the portrait.

Places to Stay on Cape Cod and the Islands

BREWSTER

Brewster by the Sea Inn
716 Main St.
(508) 896-3910
brewsterbythesea.com

Candleberry Inn
1882 Main St.
(508) 841-3505
candleberryinn.com

Old Manse Inn
1861 Main St.
(508) 896-3149
oldmanseinn.com

CHATHAM

The Chatham Inn
359 Main St.
(508) 945-9232
chathaminn.com

The Chatham Motel
1487 Main St.
(508) 945-2630
chathammotel.com

DENNIS

An English Garden Bed & Breakfast
32 Inman Rd.
(508) 398-2915
anenglishgardenbb.com

Pelham House Resort
14 Sea St.
(508) 398-6076
pelhamhouseresort.com

Sesuit Harbor House
1421 Main St.
(508) 385-3326
sesuitharborhouse.com

FALMOUTH

Palmer House Inn
81 Palmer Ave.
(508) 548-1230
palmerhouseinn.com

Red Horse Inn
28 Falmouth Heights Rd.
(508) 548-0053
redhorseinncapecod.com

Tree House Lodge
527 Woods Hole Rd.
(508) 548-1986
mytreehouselodge.com

HYANNIS

Anchor In
1 South St.
(508) 257-7127
anchorin.com

Sea Coast Inn
33 Ocean St.
(508) 775-3828
seascapecod.com

MARTHA'S VINEYARD

Beach Plum Inn
50 Beach Plum Ln.
Menemsha
(508) 645-9454
beachpluminn.com

Kelley House
23 Kelley St.
(508) 627-7900
thekelleyhousehotel.com

Nobnocket Boutique Inn
60 Mount Aldworth Rd.
Vineyard Haven
(508) 696-0859
nobnocket.com

NANTUCKET

Cliff Lodge
9 Cliff Rd.
(508) 228-9481
clifflodgenantucket.com

Hotel Pippa
5 Chestnut St.
(508) 228-5300
hotelpippa.com

Martin House Inn
61 Centre St.
(508) 228-0678
martinhouseinn.net

Nantucket Inn
1 Miller Ln.
(844) 622-0994
Nantucketinn.net

ORLEANS

Parsonage Inn
202 Main St.
(774) 722-7403
parsonageinn.com

Ships Knees Inn
186 Beach Rd.
(508) 255-1312
shipskneesinn.com

Skaket Beach Motel
203 Cranberry Hwy.
(508) 255-1020
skaketbeachmotel.com

PROVINCETOWN

AWOL
49 Provincelands Rd.
(508) 413-9820
larkhotels.com

Eben House
90 Bradford St.
(508) 487-0386
ebenhouse.com

Inn at Cook Street
7 Cook St.
(508) 252-8994
innatcookstreet.com

SANDWICH

Belfry Inn & Bistro
6 Jarves St.
(508) 888-8550
belfryinn.com

Daniel Webster Inn
149 Main St.
(855) 770-4491
danlwebsterinn.com

Isaiah Jones Homestead Bed & Breakfast
165 Main St.
(508) 888-9115
isaiahjones.com

Sandwich Inn and Suites
14 State Route 6A
(508) 888-0409
sandwichinnandsuites.com

WELLFLEET

Endless Coast
2068 Route 6
(508) 349-2530
endlesscoast.com

West Harwich
Platinum Pebble
186 Belmont Rd.
(508) 432-7766
platinumpebble.com

YARMOUTH

Bluebird Parker Beach
192 S. Shore Dr.
(508) 694-7688
bluebirdhotels.com

Chapter House Cape Cod
277 Main St.
(508) 362-4348
chapterhousecapecod.com

Liberty Hill Inn
77 Main St.
(508) 362-3976
libertyhillinn.com

Places to Eat on Cape Cod and the Islands

BREWSTER

Chillingsworth
2449 Main St.
(508) 896-3640
chillingsworth.com
Fine dining

Freeman's Grill
1000 Freeman's Way
(774) 212-3346
freemansgrill.com
American

Kitchen Café
2671 Main St.
(774) 323-0244
thekitchencafebrewster.com
Breakfast/lunch

Snowy Owl Coffee Roasters
2624 Main St.
(774) 323-0605
socoffee.co
Coffeehouse

Spinnaker
2019 Main St.
(508) 896-7644
spincape.com
Contemporary

CHATHAM

Corner Store
1403 Old Queen Anne Rd.
(508) 432-1077
chathamcornerstore.com
Mexican

Del Mar Bar & Bistro
907 Main St.
(508) 945-9988
delmarbistro.com
American

Hanger B
240 George Ryder Rd.
(508) 593-3655
hangarbcapecod.com
Breakfast/lunch

Marion's Pie Shop
2022 Main St.
(508) 432-9439
marionspieshopofchatham.com
Pie

DENNIS

The Pheasant
905 State Route 6A
(508) 385-2133
pheasantcapecod.com
American farm-to-table

Sesuit Harbor Café
357 Sesuit Neck Rd.
(508) 385-6134
sesuit-harbor-cafe.com
Seafood

Three Fins Coffee Roasters
581 Main St.
(508) 619-3372
threefinscoffee.com
Coffeehouse

FALMOUTH

Glass Onion
37 N. Main St.
(508) 540-3730
theglassoniondining.com
New American

Maison Villatte
267 Main St.
(774) 255-1855
French bakery/sandwiches

Moonakis Café
460 Waquoit Hwy.
(508) 457-9630
moonakiscafe.com
Breakfast/Lunch

Quick's Hole Taqueria
6 Luscombe Ave.
Woods Hole
(508) 495-0792
quicksholetaqueria.com
Tacos

Water Street Kitchen
86 Water St.
Woods Hole
(508) 540-5656
waterstreetkitchen.com

HYANNIS

Chez Antoine
375 Main St.
(774) 470-2180
orderchezantoinecafe.com
French/Belgian bakery

Finn's Craft Beer Tap House
16 Barnstable Rd.
(508) 534-9756
finnscraftbeertaphouse
.com
Brewpub

Pain D'Avignon
15 Hinkley Rd.
(508) 778-8588
paindavignon.com
French

Pizza Barbone
390 Main St.
(508) 957-2377
pizzabarbone.com
Pizza

Sea Street Café
50 Sea Street
(508) 534-9129
seastcafe.com
Breakfast all day

Spanky's Clam Shack
138 Ocean St.
(508) 771-2770
spankysclamshack.com
Seafood

MARTHA'S VINEYARD

Barn Bowl & Bistro
13 Uncas Ave.
Vineyard Haven
(508) 696-9800
thebarnmv.com
American

Beach Road
79 Beach Rd.
Vineyard Haven
(508) 693-8582
beachroadmv.com
Farm-to-table

Behind the Bookstore
46 Main St.
Edgartown
(774) 549-9123
btbmv.com
All-day café

Larsen's Fish Market
56 Basin Rd.
Menemsha
(508) 645-2680
larsensfishmarket.com
Seafood

Off Shore Ale
30 Kennebec Ave.
Oak Bluffs
(508) 693-2626
offshoreale.com
Brewpub

Rockfish
11 North Water St.
Edgartown
(508) 627-9967
rockfishedgartown.com
American gastropub

Scottish Bakehouse
977 State Rd.
Vineyard Haven
(508) 693-6633
scottishbakehousemv.com
Bakery café

NANTUCKET

b-Ack Yard BBQ
20 Straight Wharf
(508) 228-0227
ackbackyard.com
Barbecue

Brotherhood Nantucket
23 Broad St.
(774) 325-5812
brotherhoodnantucket.com
American

CRU Oyster Bar
One Straight Wharf
(508) 228-9278
crunantucket.com
Seafood

Handlebar Nantucket
15 Washington St.
(508) 825-5929
handlebarnantucket.com
Coffee

Lemon Press
41 Main St.
(508) 228-3800
lemonpressnantucket.com
Mediterranean

Millie's
326 Madaket Rd.
(508) 228-8435
milliesnantucket.com
Mexican/coastal

Ventuno
21 Federal St.
(508) 228-4242
ventunorestaurant.com
Italian

OTHER ATTRACTIONS

Aquinnah Cliffs
31 Aquinnah Circle
Aquinnah

Cape Cod Museum of Art
60 Hope Ln.
Dennis
(508) 896-3867
ccmnh.org

Cape Cod Museum of Natural History
869 Main St.
Brewster
(508) 896-3867
ccmnh.org

Cisco Brewers
5 Bartlett Farm Rd.
(508) 325-5929
ciscobrewers.com

Hyannis Whale Watcher Cruises
269 Millway Rd.
Barnstable
(800) 287-0374
whales.net

John F. Kennedy Hyannis Museum
397 Main St.
Hyannis
(508) 790-3077
jfkhyannismuseum.org

Martha's Vineyard Gingerbread Houses
80 Trinity Park
Oak Bluffs
(508) 693-5042
mvcma.org

Monomoy Island Excursions
731 Route 28
Harwich Port
(508) 430-7772
monomoysealcruise.com

Nantucket Whaling Museum
13 Broad St.
Nantucket
(508) 228-1894
nha.org

Pilgrim Monument Provincetown Art Museum
1 High Pole Hill Rd.
Provincetown
(508) 487-1310
Pilgrim-monument.org

ORLEANS

Abroad
89 Old Colony Way
(774) 207-0406
abroadcapecod.com
World cuisine

Cibo
15 Cove Rd.
(774) 207-0541
cibocapecod.com
Italian

Cooke's Seafood
1 South Orleans Rd.
(508) 255-5518
cookesorleans.com
Seafood

The Knack
5 State Route 6A
(774) 316-4595
theknackcapecod.com
Burgers/sandwiches/ice cream

PROVINCETOWN

Harbor Lounge
359 Commercial St.
(508) 413-9527
theharborlounge.com
Cocktails with a view

Lewis Brothers Homemade Ice Cream
310 Commercial St.
(508) 487-0977
lewisbrothersicecream.com
Ice cream

SELECTED CHAMBER OF COMMERCE & TOURISM BUREAUS

Cape Cod Chamber of Commerce
5 Patti Page Way
Centreville 02632
(508) 362-3225
capecodchamber.org

Martha's Vineyard Chamber of Commerce
24 Beach St.
Vineyard Haven 02568
(508) 693-0085
mvy.com

Nantucket Visitors Service
25 Federal St.
Nantucket 02554
(508) 228-0925
visitnantucketisland.com

Provincetown Office of Tourism
330 Commercial St.
Provincetown 02657
(774) 538-5668
ptowntourism.com

Liz's Café, Anybody's Bar
31 Bradford St.
(508) 413-9131
lizscafeptown.com
American

Lobster Pot
321 Commercial St.
(508) 487-0842
ptownlobsterpot.com
Seafood

Mac's Seafood
85 Shank Painter Rd.
(508) 487-6227
macsseafood.com
Seafood

The Mews
429 Commercial St.
(508) 487-0842
mewsptown.com
American

Nor'East Beer Garden
206 Commercial St.
(508) 487-2337
thenoreastbeergarden.com
Craft beer/small bites

Sal's Place
99 Commercial St.
(508) 487-1279
salsplaceprovincetown.com
Italian

Yolqueria
401½ Commercial St.
(508) 498-0600
yolqueria.com
Breakfast/tacos

SANDWICH

Brown Jug
155 Main St.
(508) 888-4609
thebrownjug.com
Pizza

Krua Khan Rose
289 Cotuit Rd.
(774) 413-9485
kruakhanrose.com
Thai

Treehouse Brewing Company
98 Town Neck Rd.
(413) 523-2367
treehousebrew.com
Brewery/food trucks

WELLFLEET

Moby Dick's Restaurant
3225 Route 6
(508) 349-9795
mobys.com
Seafood

PB Boulangerie Bistro
15 Lecount Hollow Rd.
(508) 349-1600
pbboulangeriebistro.com
French bakery and bistro

YARMOUTH

Keltic Kitchen
415 Route 28
(508) 771-4835
keltickitchen.com
Irish breakfast/lunch

Worcester County

Known as the "heart of the commonwealth," Worcester County is located in the center of the state, sharing a southern border with both Rhode Island and Connecticut and stretching as far north as New Hampshire. You'll be doing a lot of driving to explore the area, as this is the largest and the second-most-populous county in the state. Except for the city of Worcester, the county is largely rural forest with a smattering of quaint history-rich New England-y towns, including Harvard and Uxbridge.

Like so many Massachusetts cities and towns, Worcester is not pronounced how it is spelled. Worcester is most definitely pronounced "wu-str"; locals may even pronounce it "wuss-stuh." Both are correct.

The most traveled route (and quickest way to travel) east to west across the region is via Interstate 90, also known as the Massachusetts Turnpike, or simply the Mass Pike. The more scenic byway is US 20, which runs parallel to the Pike. Here the trees are dense, and you will see evidence of the area's agriculture past and present with orchards and farm stands on the side of the road.

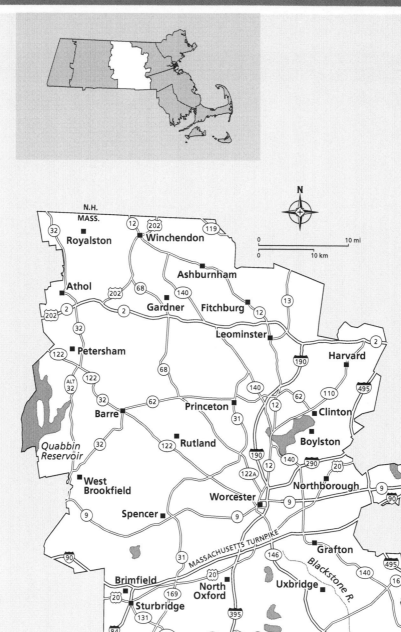

N

N.H.
MASS.

Royalston

Winchendon

Ashburnham

Athol

Gardner

Fitchburg

Leominster

Harvard

Petersham

Barre

Princeton

Clinton

Quabbin
Reservoir

Rutland

Boylston

West
Brookfield

Worcester

Northborough

Spencer

Grafton

Brimfield

North
Oxford

Uxbridge

Blackstone R.

Sturbridge

MASSACHUSETTS TURNPIKE

Webster Lake

MASS.
CONN.

MASS.

R.I.

0   10 mi
0   10 km

AUTHOR'S TOP TEN PICKS

Blackstone River and Canal Heritage Park
287 Oak St.
Uxbridge
(508) 278-7604
mass.gov/locations/blackstone-river-and-canal-heritage-state-park

Fruitlands
102 Prospect Hill Rd.
Harvard
(978) 456-3924
thetrustees.org

Museum of Russian Icons
203 Union St.
Clinton
(978) 598-5000
museumofrussianicons.org

New England Botanic Garden at Tower Hill
11 French Dr.
Boylston
(508) 869-6111
nebg.org

Old Sturbridge Village
1 Old Sturbridge Village Rd.
Sturbridge
(800) 733-1830
osv.org

Polar Park
100 Madison St.
Worcester
(508) 500-1000
milb.com/worcester

Purgatory Chasm State Reservation
198 Purgatory Rd.
Sutton
(508) 234-3733
mass.gov/locations/purgatory-chasm-state-reservation

Wachusett Mountain State Reservation
345 Mountain Rd.
Princeton
(978) 464-2987
mass.gov

Worcester Historical Museum
30 Elm St.
Worcester
(508) 753-8278
worcesterhistory.org

Worcester Public Market
152 Green St.
Worcester
(774) 366-6633
worcesterpublicmarket.org

Note: Treasure hunting at the Brimfield Antique Show? Brimfield is Worcester County–adjacent, as it is technically in neighboring Hampshire County, but it is included here because Sturbridge, which is part of Worcester Country, is just five miles from the show fields and serves as the gateway city to the whole Brimfield experience.

Worcester

Just forty-five miles from Boston, New England's second-largest city is often overlooked.

TOP ANNUAL EVENTS

SEPTEMBER

Johnny Appleseed Arts & Cultural Festival
Leominster
City Hall Plaza
(978) 660-2313

stART on the Street
Worcester
Park Ave.
Startonthestreet.org

Sterling Fair
Sterling
Sterling Airport
122 Greenland Rd.
sterlingfair.org

OCTOBER

Oktoberfest
Princeton
Wachusett Mountain Ski Area
(978) 464-2300
wachusett.com

DECEMBER

Christmas by Candlelight
Sturbridge
Old Sturbridge Village
(800) 733-1830
osv.org

In the late 1800s Worcester was an industrial boomtown, manufacturing goods as diverse as machine tools, wire, and power looms. Factory work declined in the second half of the twentieth century, and post-manufacturing gloom took over. Fast-forward to the present, and Worcester is on the rise. The city is home to nine colleges and universities, including Holy Cross, Worcester Polytech, and the University of Massachusetts Medical School. Of late, downtown has been razed and rebuilt. Much of the renaissance has been powered by the Boston Red Sox. The Sox Triple-A team relocated to Worcester in 2021, fueling development of the city's Canal District with a new stadium, hotels, and trendy eateries. There is no doubt that the Worcester Red Sox, affectionately known as the Woo Sox, has been a total home run for the city.

In the "Why have I not heard this before" category, Worcester is tops. The first public reading of the Declaration of Independence didn't take place in Boston—it happened in Worcester on the steps of South Church on July 24, 1776. The first American-made

trivia

Many Massachusetts cities have names that harken back to the English Puritan settlers' hometowns from across the pond: Boston, Cambridge, Worcester, Dedham, etc. There are, in fact, more than one hundred English place-names throughout the commonwealth (yet another British designation)—more than any other state.

mass-produced Valentine's Day cards were manufactured by Worcester's Esther Howland. And the iconic yellow Smiley Face that is the city's unofficial emblem is thanks to Harvey Ball, a local graphic designer and adman, who invented the symbol to boost employee morale for an insurance company. Take a deep dive into these Worcester firsts and many more at the ***Worcester Historical Museum*** (508-753-8278; worcesterhistory.org). The museum, located at 30 Elm Street, is open Tuesday through Saturday from 10 a.m. to 4 p.m. Admission is $5 for adults and free for children. The museum also owns the nearby Salisbury Mansion at 40 Highland Street, which dates from 1772 and shows life as it was lived by three generations of Salisburys, Worcester's "first family."

The ***Miss Worcester Diner*** (508-753-5600; missworcesterdiner.com) sits hard at 300 Southbridge Street, in the shadow of the Worcester Lunch Car Company factory where it was built in 1948. From 1906 through 1951, the Worcester Lunch Car Company turned out more than six hundred gleaming steel-and-glass diners that catered to the shift workers in New England's mill towns. The kitchen crew behind the marble countertop serve up classic breakfast and lunch diner fare at very reasonable prices. The crunchy French toast is their signature breakfast dish, while the lunchtime sandwich of choice is the pastrami and Swiss melt on rye.

There is a new team in town, and Worcester couldn't be happier about it. It has been a long road, but the Red Sox Triple-A affiliate minor league team has finally relocated from Pawtucket to their new home at ***Polar Park*** (508-500-1000; milb.com/worcester). Experience the passion that is Red Sox Nation by attending a Woo Sox game. Polar Park is a stunner of a ballpark; it's large enough to feel like the big leagues yet, with a seating capacity of just ten thousand, is small enough to watch—and maybe even meet—one of the future stars of the game. In a nod to the importance of diners to Worcester's cultural identity, a refurbished 1940s lunch car, the Sherwood Diner is adjacent to the park. Beantown Betty, a Boston Duck Tours boat that was part of the Red Sox World Series rolling rallies, has retired and is living her best life in the Polar Park outfield. Tickets are very affordable, with prices as low as $9, and concessions are largely local. Worcester favorite Coney Island Hot Dogs has the

trivia

Polar Park is named for Polar Beverages, which has been making sparkling seltzer in Worcester since 1882. Polar's bubbly water has always been popular in the region, with flavors like Cranberry Lime and Blueberry Lemonade. Recently, the brand has been riding the flavored sparkling water trend with some very un–New England flavors like Dragon Fruit Lemonade and cult favorite Unicorn Kisses.

trivia

What's the story behind *Bancroft Tower*? The granite medieval-like castle at the crest of Bancroft Tower Road in Salisbury Park was funded in 1900 by businessman Stephen Salisbury to honor Worcester native George Bancroft (1800–1891), his father's childhood friend. Bancroft did Worcester proud—he was secretary of the Navy under James Polk, delivered the eulogy at Abraham Lincoln's funeral, and served as a diplomat to both England and Germany. The fifty-six-foot tower is only open to the public on Sunday during the month of October, but it does make a great photo op year-round.

biggest presence—and the longest lines. Polar Park is in the Canal District at 100 Madison Street.

Almost directly across the street from Polar Park, at 153 Green Street, is the *Table Talk Pie Store* (508-438-1526; tabletalkpie.com). Table Talk's four-inch snack pies in the red-and-white box have been a lunch box staple for generations of New Englanders. Made in Worcester since 1924, and still a family-run business, Table Talk manufactures 250 million pies a year in several sizes and many flavors, including apple, cherry, and seasonal pecan and pumpkin. The pies at this outlet store are straight out of the oven but less than perfect; with prices as low as 50 cents for a snack pie and $2 for a full pie, you won't mind.

The stately three-story brick building at 185 Salisbury Street is the home of the *American Antiquarian Society* (508-755-5221; americanantiquarian .org), one of the country's preeminent research libraries of American history. This collection of books, newspapers and magazines and other artifacts traces American history from the first European settlement through the 1870s and the end of Reconstruction. For American history obsessives—this is your place. The society was founded in 1812 by Patriot printer Isaiah Thomas. His

Worcester Public Library

The monument in front of the Worcester Public Library at Salem Square is a fitting tribute to a trailblazing athlete who has been somewhat lost to history. The 2008 sculpture by artist Antonio Tobias Mendez honors *Marshall "Major" Taylor*, the 1899 world cycling champion. Taylor was the first African American world champion cyclist and the second Black athlete to win a world championship in any sport. Born in 1878 and raised in Indiana, he was persuaded to move to Worcester at age eighteen to train as a professional cyclist. At the turn of the twentieth century, bicycling rivaled baseball as America's most popular spectator sport. Taylor broke many racial barriers at the height of the Jim Crowe era, becoming one of America's first Black sports heroes.

personal library of seven thousand books formed the basis of the collection, and his printing press has a place of honor overlooking the Reading Room. "Old Number One" was used to print *The Massachusetts Spy*, one of the most widely circulated Revolutionary War–era newspapers and among the first to report a firsthand account of the Battle of Lexington and Concord. Also among the society's vast holdings is the first book printed in North America, a copy of the Book of Psalms, printed in Cambridge in 1640. Principally a research library, the society has a robust program of public lectures and readings that are open to the public. But your best bet to visit the society is to take one of their free public tours, offered every Wednesday at 3 p.m.

Perhaps there is no surer sign of Worcester's resurgence than the 2020 opening of the **Worcester Public Market** (774-366-6633; worcesterpublicmar ket.org), located at 152 Green Street in Kelley Square. There are thirty-six (and counting) local, independently owned vendors, all with a focus on artisanal food and specialty products. Feast on global flavors like Jamaican jerk chicken from One Love Café, Peruvian food from Pacha Mama, and Nepali food at Momo Palace. Find hyperlocal burgers at Burger Bah—there is a burger varia-tion for each of the seven hills of Worcester. Local favorite Wachusett Brewery has the biggest space—and an outdoor patio too. Among the retail offerings are Alan James for handcrafted leather goods, Sweet Life chocolates, and Stillman's Farm for produce. Market hours are Sunday, Wednesday, and Thursday from 11 a.m. to 8 p.m. and Friday and Saturday from 11 a.m. to 9 p.m.

Just a few miles southwest of Worcester, the small town of Oxford is notable as the birthplace of proto feminist and founder of the American Red Cross Clara Barton. As a young woman, Barton worked as a teacher, eventually establishing two schools. Later, she was called on to take her nursing skills to the Civil War battlefields in Maryland and Virginia. Barton's founding of the Red Cross was very much a second act—she founded the organization at age sixty and then served as its president for twenty-three years. All in all, an astonishing career for a nineteenth-century woman. The **Clara Barton Birthplace** (508-987-2056; claraburtonbirthplace.org) is located at 66 Clara Barton Road and is open late May through August, Friday through Sunday from 10 a.m. to 4 p.m. Admission is $7 for adults and $3 for children.

The recent national park status of the Blackstone River Valley National Heritage Corridor has brought an influx of new visitors and interest to this largely unknown part of Worcester County and is well worth a detour. The Blackstone River Canal is a waterway that was dug in the 1820s from Worcester to Providence, linking the cities and allowing goods to be transported cheaply and efficiently by packet ship. Indeed, the Blackstone River Canal was the high-way of its time. The canal's creation led to a boom in water-powered textile

Blackstone Valley

The Blackstone River Valley stretches from Worcester to Providence and is known as the birthplace of the Industrial Revolution. The Blackstone River and Canal Heritage Park in Uxbridge brings to light the region's manufacturing history. Purgatory Chasm in Sutton is a firm favorite of nature enthusiasts who enjoy a bit of rock climbing with their hiking.

Just off State Route 30 in the tiny town of Grafton, the *Willard Clock Museum* (508-839-3500; willardhouse.org) is probably better known nationally among watch and clock collectors than it is within Massachusetts. Clocks are a wonderful example of early scientific instruments, and early clockmakers were respected as crafts-men and engineering entrepreneurs. The clock business flourished throughout eighteenth-century New England as the result of a growing, prosperous middle class. For horologists, the Willards of Grafton are a name to know. In 1716 Joseph Willard was one of Grafton's first settlers; with time (pun intended) his four grandsons, Benjamin, Simon, Ephraim, and Aaron, established a clockmaking workshop on the property. The family's first clocks date from 1766. By 1780 much of the business had moved to Boston to better cater to their wealthy clients and to have better access to the harbor for importing the mahogany they needed for the casework. Willard Clocks were produced in Boston until the 1850s. Simon Willard is credited with designing the "banjo clock"—a smaller, more affordable wall clock that could be mass-produced. The museum showcases one of the largest collections of antique Willard clocks as well as the original Willard workshop. The museum is on the rolling farmland of the original homestead at 11 Willard Street. One-hour guided tours are offered Tuesday through Saturday at 10:30 a.m. and 2 p.m. Admission is $10 for adults, $9 for seniors, and $6 for children age thirteen and over.

factories in small towns up and down the river, transitioning the area from farming to industrialization. Uxbridge was the halfway point in the two-day river journey between Worcester and Providence, and the **Blackstone River and Canal Heritage Park** and **River Bend Visitor Center** (508-278-7604; mass.gov/locations/blackstone-river-and-canal-heritage-state-park) at 287 Oak Street, is a good starting point for exploring what was once the busiest and hardest-working river in America. The towpath trail is an easy three-mile out-and-back walk along packed gravel that brings you along the canal to view photo-friendly stone bridges and the remnants of the series of stone locks once used to allow the boats to navigate the elevation changes between the cities.

Off State Route 146 in nearby Sutton, **Purgatory Chasm State Reserva-tion** (508-234-3733; mass.gov/locations/purgatory-chasm-state-reservation) is an awe-inspiring geological wonder, a quarter-mile chasm carved in the earth over millennia from the expansion of glacial water and ice that piled granite boulders and debris across the landscape. Charley's Loop is the easy one-mile family-friendly trail option that winds through the woods. Up for a challenge? The one-mile looping Chasm Loop Trail includes some moderate inclines and a fair amount of scrambling. Features along the way include Devil's Pulpit, Lover's Leap, and the aptly named Fat Man's Misery (don't get stuck!). The visitor center is at 198 Purgatory Road. Parking fees are $5 for Massachusetts residents, $20 for nonresidents.

"Downtown" Sutton is also home to the headquarters of **Vaillancourt Folk Art** (508-476-3601; valfa.com). Founded in 1984, this made-in-Massachusetts artisan factory produces hand-painted chalkware figurines and Christmas ornaments using vintage molds. The retail gallery, museum, and art studio are located at 9 Main Street, and you might just meet one of the local artisans who

Sturbridge Townships

Historically, Sturbridge has served as a crossroads for the region. The area was known as Tantiusques to the Nipmuc people traveling between the Connecticut River Valley and the Atlantic coast. Colonists named the town Sturbridge after Stourbridge, England, and used the Native pathway to settle westward. In colonial times, Sturbridge was a popular stagecoach stop between Boston and New York. Today, Sturbridge serves much the same function, as the junction of US 20, the Massachusetts Turnpike, and Interstate 84 runs through the center of town.

Just thirty minutes outside of Worcester, experience New England life in the past tense at *Old Sturbridge Village* (800-733-1830; osv.org). Set on a landscape of two hundred acres, a cluster of forty preserved structures help tell the story of rural New England life when the nation was young. You'll be strolling right into New England village life of the 1830s with its gristmill, barns, school, and tavern. Watch a weaver, blacksmith, or cobbler demonstrate their craft using hand tools and age-old techniques. Costumed historians are on hand throughout the village to answer questions and provide insight. The village address is 1 Old Sturbridge Road. The museum is open April through December and additional weeks in winter; check the website for exact days and times. Admission is $28 for adults, $14 for children ages four through seventeen.

The *Brimfield Antique Fair* (brimfieldantiquemarket.com) is a behemoth, with approximately six thousand vendors in tents on acres of fields up and down US 20 in Brimfield. The market has a little bit of everything but is best known for its selection of antique and vintage furniture, as well as every type of collectible. Brimfield takes place three times a year—in May, July, and September—and each show runs for six days, from Tuesday through Sunday. It can be overwhelming, so it's best to have a few things in mind (architectural salvage, milk ware, Pendleton blankets) and a budget. Also, wear comfortable and, most important, closed-toe shoes; the fields are either dusty or muddy—sometime both in the same day.

brings these family heirlooms to life. Open Monday through Saturday from 9 a.m. to 5 p.m., Sunday from 10 p.m. to 5 p.m.

North Central

This part of Worcester County is Johnny Appleseed Country. John Chapman, known as Johnny Appleseed, was born in these parts, in the town of Leominster, on September 26, 1774. Come fall, the orchard towns of Harvard, Stow, and Northborough are apple-picking central. At two thousand feet, Princeton's Wachusett Mountain is the region's highest peak and boasts views of distant apple orchards, the Berkshire Hills, and, on a clear day, Boston. Winter, though, is Wachusett's season to shine, bringing an onslaught of day-trippers for skiing. Nearby, Ashburnham and Clinton are no longer drive-through mill towns; each is home to a singular museum—grand pianos and Russian icons, respectively—that attract visitors from around the world. Boylston practically abuts Worcester and is home to the New England Botanic Garden at Tower Hill, which is open year-round and a must-visit for plant lovers.

A lovely drive along State Route 2 through the countryside brings the ever-charming town of Harvard and the marvelously eclectic **Fruitlands Museum** (978-456-3924; thetrustees.org).

Situated on 210 pastoral acres in the Nashoba River Valley, Fruitlands was originally founded as a Utopian Transcendentalist community in the 1840s by Bronson Alcott, father of Louisa May Alcott, who later wrote critically of her experience. Fruitlands was named to reflect the tenet of living "off the fruit of the land," but it was a rather short-lived experiment in self-reliance—the community failed after just seven months. As a museum, the property was founded in 1914 and showcases the original Fruitlands farmhouse, a Shaker Museum of crafts and furniture, a Native American Museum, and a Museum of Art. The Museum of Art is particularly noteworthy for its fifty Hudson River School landscapes; there is an exceptional Albert Bierstadt, *Mt. Ascutney from Claremont*, which features a postcard-pretty scene of cattle and sheep grazing in the foothills of a New Hampshire farm. There are four miles of looping, well-marked walking trails throughout the property. In winter the museum actively encourages sledding and cross-country skiing (bring your own) as well as snowshoeing (rentals are available). The on-site **Hyve Café** offers light meals with ingredients from area farms; it is very good and reasonably priced. The museum is located at 102 Prospect Hill Road and is open April through November, Monday and Wednesday through Friday from 10 a.m. to 4 p.m., Saturday and Sunday from 10 a.m. to 5 p.m.; closed on Tuesday. Admission is $12 for adults and $6 for children. The grounds are open year-round.

The back roads of Worcester County are scattered with apple orchards. One of the very best is **Tougas Family Farm** (508-393-6406; tougasfamilyfarm.com), located at the top of Ball Street in Northborough. The ninety-acre farm is open June through October for pick-your-own fruit. The season starts with strawberries, followed by cherries, raspberries, blueberries, and blackberries. The you-pick season really gets going in August; if you hit it just right, you can pick peaches, raspberries, and early apples on the same day. For the little ones, there is a playground and a barn with goats and lambs and wagon rides to the fields on the weekends. Their farm stand and kitchen offer picked fruit for sale as well as ice cream, drinks, and pie. Apple picking also means picking up apple cider doughnuts—warm-from-the-oven Tougas cider doughnuts are heavenly.

New England Botanic Garden at Tower Hill (508-869-6111; nebg.org) is one of the lesser-known garden oases in the region. Set in sleepy Boylston at 11 French Drive, the 170-acre garden was created in 1842 by the Worcester County Horticultural Society. Highlights include a bold and bright cottage garden and a vegetable garden, as well as extensive landscaped grounds, including an apple orchard, woods, and meadows. It's rather a wonderful place for gardening inspiration. In the spring, the garden really shows off. If it's chilly, take refuge in the two conservatories to check out the exotics. The on-site **Farmer and the Fork Café** has an eclectic menu that features fresh and locally sourced ingredients, some picked on-site. The garden is open daily from 10 a.m. to 5 p.m. Admission is $18 for adults, $15 for seniors, $8 for children ages four through twelve, and $7 for dogs (canine admission is a rarity in these parts).

A secret no more, Clinton's **Museum of Russian Icons** (978-598-5000; museumofrussianicons.org) holds the largest private collection of Russian icons outside the motherland. The museum is the vision of founder Gordon Lankton, who has created a world-class cultural destination in this old factory town. The extraordinary collection spans six centuries of Russian iconography—a form of sacred art, usually egg tempera on wood, that is distinguished by its vivid colors and gold leaf. The museum's Russian tearoom is a lovely spot for light refreshments. The museum is located at 203 Union Street and is open Thursday

trivia

Just four miles from Clinton, the tiny village of Sterling was the hometown of Mary Sawyer, of "Mary Had a Little Lamb" fame. Sawyer was born in 1806 on the family's Sterling farm. Young Mary brought the lamb to school one day, and the rest, as they say, is history. A statue of a lamb on the Sterling Common at Meetinghouse Hill Road commemorates Mary, her pet, and the story.

through Sunday from 10 a.m. to 4 p.m. Admission is $12 for adults and free for children age thirteen and under.

One of the area's best year-round hikes is practically in Worcester's back yard. It's just a thirty-minute drive to *Wachusett Mountain State Park* (978-464-2987; mass.gov). Wachusett has a large trail system, so pick up a map from the visitor center at 345 Mountain Road before heading out. The one-mile looping Pine Hill Trail to the summit is moderately challenging, but is worth the climb. On a clear day you can see the Boston skyline to the east and New Hampshire's Mount Monadnock to the north. You can also drive to the summit when the access road is open, which is generally May through October. Parking fees are $5 for Massachusetts residents, $20 for nonresidents.

Wachusett Mountain (978-464-2300; wachusett.com) is easily Massachusetts's most popular ski area. It's the closest ski mountain to Boston, or, as their rather catchy jingle says, "Wa-wa-chusett; mountain skiing minutes away." Wachusett has both downhill skiing and snowboarding, with twenty-six trails and eight lifts and nearly complete snowmaking. Wachusett is a family-owned mountain that caters to kids with a well-regarded learn-to-ski program, plenty of beginner trails, and an awesome post-and-beam base lodge that offers tons of food options. The parking lot address is 41 Mile Hill Road.

A former brick library in the mill town of Ashburnham is an unlikely place to find a collection of antique grand pianos. The *Frederick Collection of Grand Pianos* (978-827-6232; frederickcollection.org) is the passion project of husband and wife Edmund and Patricia Frederick. The collection includes more than twenty pianos ranging from a 1790s Viennese instrument to a 1928 Parisian Erard. These pianos are not just museum pieces. Each instrument has its own tone and its own voice, and they are frequently played by both amateur and professional musicians, allowing listeners to enjoy music on the instrument as it was intended by the composer.

If you can hold your own, you will be invited to play. Otherwise, Edmund or Patricia will demonstrate the sound characteristics of some of the pianos, starting from the more modern and working back to some of the oldest. Tours are highly personalized depending on interest, and can last two to three hours. Musicians and music lovers typically do not mind in the slightest.

The pianos are kept in top playing condition and are used for performances and recitals by some of the world's most renowned soloists. The Fredericks host an annual Historical Piano Concert Series (check the website for schedule) held at the Ashburnham Community Church at 84 Main Street. The museum is at 30 Main Street and is open Thursday and Saturday from 10 a.m. to 4 p.m., or by arrangement. Admission is free, but donations are gratefully accepted.

SELECTED CHAMBERS OF COMMERCE & TOURISM BUREAUS

Blackstone Valley Chamber of Commerce
670 Linwood Ave.
Whitinsville 01588
(508) 234-9090
blackstonevalley.org

Discover Central Massachusetts
311 Main St.
Worcester 01608
(508) 753-1550
discovercentralma.org

Sturbridge Tourist Association
308 Main St.
Sturbridge 01566
(508) 347-2500
sturbridge.gov

Wachusett Area Chamber of Commerce
1179 Main St.
Holden 01520
(508) 829-9220
wachusettareachamber.org

OTHER ATTRACTIONS

Ecotarium
222 Harrington Way
Worcester
(508) 928-2700
ecotarium.org

Fitchburg Art Museum
185 Elm St.
Fitchburg
(978) 345-4207
fitchburgartmuseum.org

Worcester Art Museum
55 Salisbury St.
Worcester
(508) 799-4406
worcesterart.org

Places to Stay in Worcester County

ASHBURNHAM

Maguire House
30 Cobb Rd.
(978) 827-5053
maguirehouse.com

STURBRIDGE

Publick House
277 Main St.
(508) 347-3313
publickhouse.com

WORCESTER

AC Hotel by Marriott Worcester
125 Front St.
(774) 420-7555
marriott.com

Beechwood Hotel
363 Plantation St.
(508) 754-5789
beechwoodhotel.com

Homewood Suites by Hilton Worcester
1 Washington Square
(855) 605-0320
hilton.com

Vida Boutique Inn
110 Vernon St.
(774) 823-3807
vidaboutiqueinn.com

Places to Eat in Worcester County

STURBRIDGE

B.T.'s Smokehouse
392 Main St.
(508) 347-3188
btsmokehouse.com
Barbecue

Cedar Street Grille
12 Cedar St.
(508) 347-5800
cedarstreetgrill.com
American

WORCESTER

Armsby Abbey
144 Main St.
(508) 795-1012
armsbyabbey.com
Gastropub

Birch Tree Bread Company
138 Green St.
(774) 243-6944
birchtreebreadcompany
.com
Bakery/café

Deadhorse Hill
281 Main St.
(774) 420-7107
deadhorsehill.com
New England farm-to-table

The Fix Burger Bar
108 Grove St.
(774) 823-3327
thefixburgerbar.com
Burgers

'Olo Pizza
40 Millbrook St.
(508) 459-1959
olopizza.com
Pizza

Sole Proprietor
118 Highland St.
(508) 798-3474
thesole.com
Seafood

WEST BROOKFIELD

Salem Cross Inn
260 Main St.
(508) 867-2345
salemcrossinn.com
New England

Pioneer Valley

The Connecticut River is New England's longest, stretching more than four hundred miles from New Hampshire to Long Island Sound. Between Worcester and the Berkshires, the Pioneer Valley is generally considered the area of the Connecticut River Valley located within Massachusetts. Largely agricultural and rural, the region includes Franklin, Hampshire, and Hampden Counties. Across the northern Pioneer Valley and extending into the Berkshires, the Mohawk Trail is one of America's first scenic auto routes; it is truly a drive to remember, with inviting stops all along the way. In the Southern Pioneer Valley, Springfield is the state's fourth-largest city and is home to both the Naismith Memorial Basketball Hall of Fame and the Dr. Seuss Museum. In between, the college towns of Amherst and Northampton offer a vibrant cultural life that centers on the "Five College Consortium": Amherst College, Hampshire College, Smith College, Mount Holyoke, and the flagship campus of the University of Massachusetts.

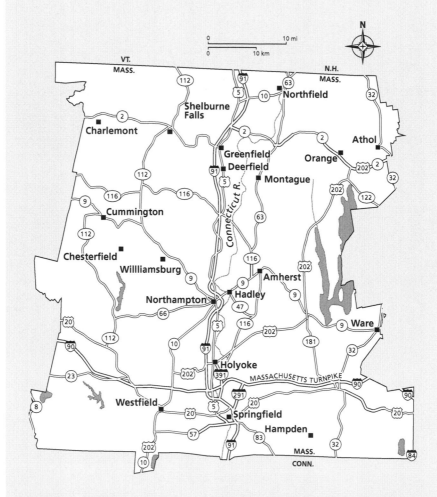

AUTHOR'S TOP TEN PICKS

Beneski Museum of Natural History
11 Barrett Hill Dr.
Amherst
(413) 542-2165
amherst.edu/museums/naturalhistory

The Botanic Garden of Smith College
16 College Ln.
Northampton
(413) 585-2742
garden.smith.edu

Bridge of Flowers
22 Water St.
Shelburne Falls
bridgeofflowersmass.org

Calvin Coolidge Presidential Library
20 West St.
Northampton
(413) 587-1011
forbeslibrary.org

Emily Dickinson House
260 Main St.
Amherst
(413) 542-8161
emily-dickinson.org

Eric Carle Museum of Picture Book Art
125 W. Bay Rd.
Amherst
(413) 559-6300
carlemuseum.org

Historic Deerfield
80 Old Main St.
Deerfield
(413) 775-7214
historic-deerfield.org

Mohawk Trail
State Route 2
Greenfield–North Adams
(413) 743-8127
mohawktrail.com

Skinner State Park
10 Skinner State Park Rd.
(413) 586-0350
Hadley
mass.gov/locations/skinner-state-park

Springfield Museums
21 Edward St.
Springfield
(413) 263-6800
springfieldmuseums.org

In spring, when the rivers are gushing, the ***Turner's Fall Fishway*** (800-859-2960) is a great spot to see the annual shad run. Just behind the Montague Town Hall at 15 First Street, visitors can see the fish from underwater viewing windows at the Cabot Hydroelectric Station as they migrate from coastal waters on their way up and over the Turner's Fall Dam to spawn upstream. The viewing windows are open mid-May through mid-June, Wednesday through Sunday from 9 a.m. to 5 p.m. Admission is free.

Take time out to stop in at ***Richardson's Candy Kitchen*** (413-772-0443; richardsonscandy.com) at 500 Greenfield Road. The shop is renowned for their dixies: caramel and nuts (pecan, walnuts, cashew, or almond) enrobed in dark or milk chocolate.

Mohawk Trail

The Mohawk Trail roughly follows the Native trading path along the Deerfield River. It is a gorgeous seventy-mile stretch of State Route 2 that runs east–west across the northern part of the state. It's an ever-changing journey of stop-and-stare vistas of verdant valleys cradled by mountains along with turnoffs that lead to orchards and sugarhouses. It is most certainly a scenic route and is an exceptional driving adventure year-round, but most especially in the fall.

The remote town of Northfield makes a great Mohawk Trail starting point as you push west, traveling the breadth of Franklin County.

This part of the Mohawk Trail is the heart of the Connecticut River Valley. At the **Northfield Mountain Recreation and Environmental Center** (413-659-3714; first lightpower.com/recreation) board the riverboat *Heritage* for a leisurely ninety-minute narrated Connecticut River cruise that travels downriver under the impressive French King Bridge, linking the tiny Franklin County towns of Erving and Gill (check website for the schedule). Rates are $15 for adults, $8 for ages fourteen and under.

Although not as well-known as some of the state's other outdoor history museums, **Historic Deerfield** (413-775-7214; historic-deerfield.org) offers a unique window into life during colonial America. The first British settlers came to farm the rich soil of this valley at the crossroads of the Deerfield and Connecticut Rivers in the 1670s. At the time, it was one of the outlying British villages of the American colonies and experienced frequent raids by the Pocumtuck. Deerfield is unique in that the town still retains its original scale and town plan and has preserved nearly sixty buildings from the eighteenth and nineteenth centuries; it is a mix of both private residences and museum buildings. Admission includes the **Flynt Center of Early New England Life**, which has taken a modern cabinet-of-curiosities approach to displaying its extensively well-documented artifact collection. Visits also include guided tours of the foundation's historic house museums along with craft demonstrations and workshops. Historic Deerfield is located at 80 Old Main Street and is open mid-April through late November, Wednesday through Sunday and Monday holidays from 9:30 a.m. to 4:30 p.m. Admission is $18 for adults, free for children age twelve and under.

Dating from 1884, the **Deerfield Inn** (413-774-5587; deerfieldinn.com) sits in the center of town at 81 Old Main

trivia

Travel writers in the 1920s and 1930s are credited with coining the name "Pioneer Valley" as a way to encourage tourism to the region as automobiles became popular and more people took to the road in search of adventure.

Street. The twenty-four guest rooms are tastefully appointed, and they are as charming as they are comfortable. Rates include continental breakfast. The on-site **Champney's Tavern** offers breakfast as well as lunch and dinner and feature a menu of classic American bar fare like burgers, fish-and-chips, and pizza.

A bit farther along State Route 2, the village of Shelburne Falls is practically a mandatory Mohawk Trail pit stop. Here, the mighty Deerfield River has created one of those geological curiosities that just appears—in this case a series of dramatic glacial granite potholes in the water.

trivia

Northfield couple Monroe and Isabel Smith opened the first American youth hostel in Northfield in December 1934 after experiencing hosteling in Europe. Within a year, the Smiths had launched thirty youth hostels throughout New England, establishing the American Youth Hostel movement.

Located on the Deerfield River in the middle of town, it seems that the craftspeople who show at the **Salmon Falls Artisan Studios** (413-625-9833; salmonfallsgallery.com) need only look out the window for artistic inspiration. The showroom/studio space is located at One Ashfield Street and hosts more than ninety artists working in all mediums, including painting, photography, wood, metal, and glass.

Shelburne's showstopper attraction is its **Bridge of Flowers** (bridgeof flowersmass.org). The town's 1908 trolley bridge spans the Deerfield River, connecting Shelburne to the town of Buckland. By 1927 the trolley had become obsolete, and the bridge was considered an eyesore. In 1929 the local women's gardening club transformed the bridge into a flowering pedestrian walkway. Nearly a century later, Shelburne's horticultural beautification project continues, with an army of volunteers ensuring that the bridge blooms in a riot of color year-round. The bridge is open twenty-four hours; there is no admission, but donations are accepted.

Just steps from the river, at 14 Depot Street, is the **Shelburne Falls Trolley Museum** (413-625-9443; sftm.org). Undoubtedly the favorite part of any visit are the trolley rides. Hop aboard No. 10, which dates from 1896 and is one of the country's oldest working trolleys. Or give the antique pumper a go along the track—it's quite a workout for those arm muscles. The museum is open from the end of May through October, Saturday and Sunday from 11 a.m. to 5 p.m. In July and August, the museum is also open on Monday from 1 p.m. to 5 p.m. Admission is $4 for adults and $2 for children.

From Shelburne, a happy choice awaits. Continue heading west along State Route 2 toward North Adams and the Berkshires. Alternatively, backtrack south along US 5 and on to the college towns of Amherst and Northampton.

TOP ANNUAL EVENTS

MARCH

Holyoke St. Patrick's Day Parade
Holyoke
holyokestpatricksday.com

APRIL

River Rat Race
Athol/Orange
riverratrace.org

JUNE

Green River Festival
Greenfield
greenriverfestival.com

Hadley Asparagus Festival
Hadley
nepm.org

JULY

Yidstock: Festival of New Yiddish Music
Amherst
(413) 256-4900
yiddishbookcenter.org

AUGUST

Springfield Jazz & Roots Festival
Springfield
springfieldjazzfest.com

SEPTEMBER

The Eastern State Exposition (The Big E)
West Springfield
(413) 737-2443
thebige.com

Franklin County Fair
Greenfield
(413) 774-4282
fcas.com

Old Deerfield Fall Craft Fair
Deerfield
(413) 774-7476
deerfield-craft.org

Three County Fair
Northampton
(413) 584-2237
3countyfair.com

OCTOBER

North Quabbin Garlic & Arts Festival
Orange
garlicandarts.org

NOVEMBER

Franklin County Cider Days
Throughout Franklin County
(413) 773-5463
ciderdays.org

DECEMBER

Bright Nights at Forest Park
Springfield
(413) 733-3800
brightnights.org

If you choose to mosey along State Route 2, the next ten miles feature farmland and thick forest. In Charlmont, **_Zoar Outdoors_** (413-339-4010; zoaroutdoor.com) offers everyone from the avid sportsman/woman to the casual nature lover a taste of the Deerfield River's exhilarating whitewater rapids. The boathouse is at 7 Main Street, and the season generally runs from April through October.

This next ten miles are firmly the middle portion of the trail, as it reaches its highest point at Mohawk Park just west of Charlmont. Turn off here to view **Hail to the Sunrise**, a towering bronze of a Mohawk man looking eastward with his arms extended. The statue dates from 1932 and at the time was considered a contemporary work of art. Today the statue is considered inaccurate as well as controversial. Will it remain?

It's another twelve miles to the **Golden Eagle Restaurant** (413-663-9834), which is located at 1935 Mohawk Trail, overlooking the trail's infamous hairpin turn. After miles of driving uphill, it's a great place to relax with a drink and marvel at the knockout panoramic view of the entire region from the dining room's windows.

Buckle up. Heading east to west saves the best for last—the final section of the road spirals down as you roll on into North Adams and the gorgeous Berkshire Hills.

Montague

You may have to backtrack east along State Route 2 to pick up US 5 south to hit the college towns of Amherst and Northampton. But any trek in this direction should include a stop in Montague to visit the legendary **Montague Book Mill** (413-367-9206; montaguebookmill.com), known throughout the area for its charming tagline: "Books you don't need in a place you can't find." The used bookstore is set in a rambling 1842 gristmill overlooking the Sawmill River.

For many book lovers, a trip through Amherst's back roads to seek out the bookstore is a challenge accepted and more than met. Comfy couches make it easy to happily while away the hours. The complex also houses the **Lady Killigrew Cafe** (413-367-9666; theladykilligrew.com), which has a menu of sandwiches, soups, salads, and bowls (get the peanut ginger udon noodles). Their nitro cold brew is quietly one of the area's best; beer and wine are available by the glass too. The address for the entire mill complex is 440 Greenfield Road.

Amherst

Amherst is a true college town and gets tremendous energy from its schools—most notably from the University of Massachusetts–Amherst, which has a student body of nearly thirty thousand. Not to be confused with UMass, Amherst College is a small liberal arts school with a graceful campus that includes the Emily Dickinson House and the Beneski Museum, one of New England's best natural history museums. Not to be overlooked, tiny Hampshire College is home to a duo of museums, including the Eric Carle Museum of Picture Book Art and the Yiddish Book Center.

The elegant buttercup-yellow brick **Emily Dickinson House** (413-542-8161; emily-dickinson.org) is where the famously reclusive poet, "The Belle of Amherst," was born in 1830 and spent most of her life. Located in the center of Amherst at 260 Main Street, the house has been immaculately preserved with original objects from the Dickinson family, including furniture and household items. On the upper floor is the sunny bedroom where Dickinson wrote letters and some 1,800 poems. A replica of her writing table (the original is at Harvard) and a copy of Dickinson's white housedress (the original is at the Amherst Historical Society) are on display. Today, Dickinson's poetry still stirs hearts and minds and her fans are legion; but her genius was unrecognized in her lifetime. The house is owned by Amherst College and is open for guided tours March through December, Tuesday through Sunday from 10 a.m. to 5 p.m. Admission is $16 for adults and free for children age seventeen and under.

At the edge of the Hampshire College campus, a vaguely Eastern European village-like group of buildings, a shtetl, is set in a small apple orchard. The **Yiddish Book Center** (413-256-4900; yiddishbookcenter.org) is dedicated to all things Yiddish. With the help of volunteers and the public, the museum has made it its mission to recover more than a million Yiddish books to help preserve Yiddish culture and tell the story of the Jewish people. The museum is located at 1021 West Street and is open Sunday through Friday from 10 a.m. to 4 p.m. There is a suggested donation of $8 for adults.

Next door to Hampshire College, at 125 West Bay Road, the **Eric Carle Museum of Picture Book Art** (413-559-6300; carlemuseum.org) showcases the artwork of the beloved children's illustrator of seventy books, including *The Very Hungry Caterpillar*. The museum also mounts fresh exhibits that celebrate the art of children's book illustration and literature. The museum is not just for children. Past exhibits have included Boundless: Picture Books About Disabilities and Read the World: Picture Books in Translation. The museum is open Wednesday through Friday from 10 a.m. to 4 p.m., Saturday from 10 a.m. to 5 p.m., and Sunday noon to 5 p.m. Admission is $9 for adults and $6 for children.

On the campus of Amherst College, the **Beneski Museum of Natural History** (413-542-2165; amherst.edu/museums/naturalhistory) is one of the largest natural history museums in New England. The strength of its collection is its dinosaur fossils, many of which were found locally in the Connecticut River Valley. But it is the largest fossil on display, the 1923 Columbian mammoth skeleton (which is also the school's mascot), that is the museum's most popular. The address of the museum is 11 Barrett Hill Drive; hours are Tuesday through Friday from 10 a.m. to 4 p.m., Saturday and Sunday from 10 a.m. to 5 p.m. Admission is free.

Hadley

Taking a short walk is a good idea while day-tripping, and the tiny nearby community of Hadley offers not one, but two leg-stretching opportunities.

English-born Thomas Cole was considered the father of what became known as the Hudson River School of Painting. View Cole's *The Oxbow* in real life at the Summit House in **Skinner State Park** (413-586-0350; mass.gov/locations/skinner-state-park). The nineteenth-century landscape oil titled *View from Mount Holyoke, Northampton, Massachusetts, after a Thunderstorm* is part of the collection of the Metropolitan Museum of Art in New York and is considered one of the most significant American landscape paintings. From the parking lot it is a one-and-a-half-mile ramble to Summit House; the shuttered landmark hotel's wraparound porch is open to visitors to enjoy the same Connecticut River view that dazzled Cole. Not in the mood to hike? Take the auto road to the top. The parking lot address is 10 Skinner State Park Road; the park road is open daily from 9 a.m. to 8 p.m.; the Summit House is open seasonally from 9 a.m. to 4 p.m. The parking fee is $5 for Massachusetts residents, $20 for nonresidents.

Take a detour to see some dinosaur footprints that are hidden in plain sight off US 5 just north of Holyoke at **Dinosaur Footprints Reservation** (413-213-4751; thetrustees.org/place/dinosaur-footprints). Follow the dirt path from the parking lot; there is an overlook area to view the Connecticut River and signs directing you to the fossil site, which was discovered in 1802 and features fossil specimens thought to be two hundred million years old. This dinosaur adventure takes less than thirty minutes—and it's free. The park is open April 1 through November 30 from dawn to dusk.

Nothing says New England more than a farm stand on the side of the road. Hadley's **Barstow's** (413-586-2142; barstowslongviewfarm.com) is a working farm that offers breakfast, lunch, and ice cream. All is best enjoyed on picnic tables outside, the herd of cows in the meadow providing wholesome dairy farm ambience.

Northampton

Northampton has a strong outdoorsy/artsy vibe that is embraced by both students and residents, with a town center that bustles with shopping, dining, and street life. Among the hot spots in town are Smith College's Botanic Garden and its Museum of Art.

The **Botanic Garden of Smith College** (413-585-2742; garden.smith.edu) is one of the few botanical gardens in the United States that encompasses the entire campus. This not only makes it a valuable resource for students but also makes the campus one of the most popular tourist attractions in the Pioneer Valley. The arboretum spans 127 acres and blooms with 1,200 species of trees, shrubs, flowers, and other plants. The glass-and-steel Lyman Conservatory is stunning, featuring nearly a dozen themed rooms that showcase plants from around the world, including palm trees as tall as the ceiling, a pond, and a showhouse that blooms with seasonal floral displays, like camellias in the winter and mums in the fall. The conservatory address is 16 College Lane. The greenhouses are open Monday through Friday from 9 a.m. to 4 p.m. Admission is by a suggested donation of $2 per person. The grounds and arboretum are open to the public daily from dawn to dusk.

In terms of "wow factor," few college art museums surpass the **Smith College Museum of Art** (413-285-2760; scma.smith.edu) a fact made all the more amazing by its remote location in Northampton. The museum's Impressionists are alone worth the price of admission (which is only $5 for adults) with works by Monet, Degas, and Van Gogh. The museum is located at 20 Elm Street and is open Tuesday through Sunday from 11 a.m. to 4 p.m.

The best Massachusetts park that no one has ever heard of may just be **Look Park** (413-584-5457; lookpark.org), a 150-acre private park located in Northampton that offers a variety of special amenities, including a pond with pedal boats, groomed walking paths, a wildlife center with fallow deer, an eighteen-hole miniature golf course, miniature steam train rides—and, count them, four separate playgrounds for the kids. Look Park is in Northampton's Florence neighborhood at 300 Main Street and is open year-round, Monday through Friday from 9 a.m. to 4 p.m., Saturday and Sunday from 9 a.m. to 6 p.m. Admission is by parking fee: $5 per car weekdays, $10 on the weekends. There are additional fees for some of the activities.

Herrell's Ice Cream (413-586-9700; herrells.com) is a pioneering ice cream shop that in the 1970s popularized "mix-ins" like crushed Heath bar and Oreos added to premium, slow-churned ice cream. The legacy lives on in Herrell's Thornes Marketplace shop at 8 Old South Street—and ice cream fans are forever grateful.

The eleven-mile **Norwottuck Rail Trail** (413-586-8706; mass.gov/loca tions/norwottuck-rail-trail) follows the route of the old Central Massachusetts Railroad, linking Northampton, Hadley, and Amherst. Pick up the trail in Northampton at State Route 9 and Damon Road, and this ride is scenic right from the start as you cross the Connecticut River biking east. The Pioneer Valley is a haven for cyclists and has many bike shops as well as a well-established bike-share system. **Northampton Bicycle** (413-586-3810; nohobike) can set you up. Or, if doing a one-way trip, consider bike-sharing with ***Valley Bike*** (877-460-2435; valleybike.org).

Sure, everybody knows that the John F. Kennedy Library is in Massachusetts, but very few know that Northampton is home to the ***Calvin Coolidge Presidential Library*** (413-587-1011; forbeslibrary.org). Forbes Library is Northampton's main public library, and it is the only presidential library that is in an actual library. Coolidge was the thirtieth president of the United States, serving from 1923 to 1929. He was a Vermonter but came to Massachusetts to attend Amherst College. He eventually opened a law office in Northampton and began his political career here, winning election as city councilor and eventually becoming mayor of Northampton, governor of Massachusetts, and vice president under Warren Harding. When Coolidge declined to seek a second presidential term, he returned to Northampton until his death four years later, in 1933. The presidential library consists of two rooms on the second floor with displays of Coolidge's personal papers, books, and family mementos. Museum highlights include Western hats and an eagle-feather headdress that was presented to Coolidge as a gift from the Sioux Nation. The library is located at 20 West Street and is open Monday through Friday from 10 a.m. to 5 p.m., Saturday from 2 p.m. to 4 p.m.

Springfield

Founded in 1636 and located on the banks of the Connecticut River, Springfield is the largest city in the Pioneer Valley and the fourth largest in the

The Lost Towns of the Quabbin

Just to the east of the Pioneer Valley, the Quabbin Reservoir is the largest inland body of water in Massachusetts. Its name means "place of many waters," and it is the principal freshwater source for much of the state. In 1938 four towns—Dana, Enfield, Greenwich, and Prescott—were disincorporated, their residents displaced, and the towns flooded to create the reservoir.

Dana, Enfield, Greenwich, and Prescott may be gone, but they are not forgotten. Curiosity seekers can even visit where the town of Dana once existed. The elevation of Dana Common was high enough so that, even after the controlled flooding, it has stayed dry. The foundations of many of the buildings that once stood here, including some homes, the town hall, and the school, remain. Dana Common is listed on the National Register of Historic Places; access to the site is at Gate 40 off State Route 32A in Petersham.

commonwealth. Springfield's big draw is its impressive collection of five world-class museums. The ***Springfield Museums*** (413-263-6800; springfieldmuseums .org) are all in one location, on the Quadrangle at 21 Edward Street, and include two art museums, a science museum, a history museum, as well as its newest institution, a museum dedicated to Theodor Seuss Geisel, more widely known as Dr. Seuss and Springfield's beloved native son. The museums are open Monday through Saturday from 10 a.m. to 5 p.m., Sunday from 11 a.m. to 5 p.m. Admission is $25 for adults, $13 for children ages three through seventeen, and includes entrance to all five museums.

The ***Swift River Museum*** (978-544-6882; swiftrivermuseum.org) is dedicated to preserving and telling the stories of the four towns lost to the Quabbin Reservoir. The museum maintains a house, a church, and a barn; all are structures from the towns that were moved intact in advance of the flooding. The museum is in New Salem at 40 Elm Street and is open by appointment late June through mid-September, Wednesday and Sunday, from 1 p.m. to 4 p.m.

Places to Stay in the Pioneer Valley

AMHERST

Allen House and Amherst Inn
599 and 257 Main St.
(413) 252-5000
allenhouse.com

Black Walnut Inn
1184 Pleasant St.
(413) 549-5694
blackwalnutinn.com

Inn on Boltwood
30 Boltwood Ave.
(413) 256-8200
innonboltwood.com

HATFIELD

Old Mill Inn
87 School St.
(413) 247-3301
oldmillinn.us

NORTHAMPTON

The Ellery Hotel
259 Elm St.
(413) 584-7660
elleryhotel.com

Hotel Northampton
36 King St.
(413) 584-3100
hotelnorthampton.com

Places to Eat in the Pioneer Valley

AMHERST

Antonio's Pizza
31 North Pleasant St.
(413) 253-0808
antoniospizza.com
Pizza

Bistro 63
63 North Pleasant St.
(413) 259-1600
bistro63.com
American

Black Sheep Deli
79 Main St.
(413) 253-3442
blacksheepdeli.com
Delicatessen

Johnny's Tavern
30 Boltwood Walk
(413) 253-8000
johnnystavernamherst.com
American

Osteria Vespa
28 Amity St.
(413) 230-3194
osteriavespa.com
Italian

HADLEY

Pulse Café
270 Russell St.
(413) 387-0555
pulsecafe.com
Vegan

NORTHAMPTON

Homestead
7 Strong Ave.
(413) 586-0502
eathomestead.com
Farm-to-table

Jake's
17 King St.
(413) 584-9613
jakesnorthampton.com
Breakfast/lunch

Northampton Brewery
11 Brewster Ct.
(413) 584-9903
northamptonbrewery.com
Brewery

Paul and Elizabeth's
150 Main St.
(413) 584-4832
paulandelizabeths.com
Seafood

SPRINGFIELD

Student Prince
8 Fort St.
(413) 734-7575
studentprince.com
German

Theodore's
201 Worthington St.
(413) 736-6000
theodoresbbq.com
Barbecue

SUNDERLAND

Blue Heron
112 N. Main St.
(413) 665-2102
blueherondining.com
American fine dining

OTHER ATTRACTIONS

International Volleyball Hall of Fame
444 Dwight St.
Holyoke
(413) 536-0926
volleyhall.org

Magic Wings Butterfly Conservatory & Gardens
281 Greenfield Rd.
South Deerfield
(413) 665-2805
magicwings.com

Naismith Memorial Basketball Hall of Fame
1000 Hall of Fame Ave.
Springfield
(877) 446-6752
hoophall.com

Six Flags New England
1623 Main St.
Agawam
(413) 786-9300
sixflags.com/newengland

Yankee Candle Village
25 Greenfield Rd.
South Deerfield
(877) 636-7707
yankeecandle.com

SELECTED CHAMBERS OF COMMERCE & TOURISM BUREAUS

Franklin County Chamber of Commerce
79 Old Main St.
Deerfield 01342
(413) 773-5463
franklincc.org

Hampshire County Tourism & Visitors Bureau
99 Pleasant St.
Northampton 01060
(413) 584-1900
visithamsphirecounty.com

Mohawk Trail Association
PO Box 1044
North Adams 01247
(413) 743-8127
mohawktrail.com

Western Massachusetts/Greater Springfield Convention & Visitors Bureau
1441 Main St.
Springfield 01103
(413) 787-1548
explorewesternmass.com

The Berkshires

The hilly hinterlands of western Massachusetts may be in the middle of nowhere. But for a lot of people, that is exactly the point. Framed by mountains halfway between Boston and New York City, there is something about these storybook forests and rolling hills dotted with lakes that has long inspired musicians, writers, and artists.

In the nineteenth and twentieth centuries, the Berkshires became popular as a summer destination for novelists Herman Melville, Nathaniel Hawthorne, and Edith Wharton and artists Daniel Chester French and Henry Hudson Kitson. As the Berkshires became a cultural center, the well-to-do followed, building "cottages"—lavish estates built as summer homes to escape the heat of the city.

The Berkshires cover quite a bit of ground. There are thirty-plus towns in the region's 950 square miles. Berkshire County spans the state's entire edge with New York, from artsy Williamstown at the Vermont border to the farmlands in the south near Connecticut.

In between, the hills are alive with the sound of the Boston Symphony Orchestra. Since the 1930s Lenox has been the summer home of the BSO. And although the Tanglewood

THE BERKSHIRES

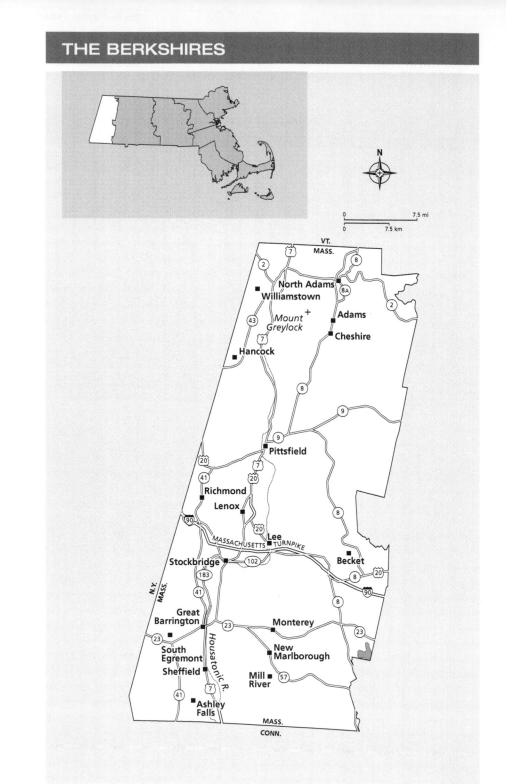

AUTHOR'S TOP TEN PICKS

The BSO at Tanglewood
297 West St.
Lenox
(617) 266-1200
bso.org

Chesterwood
4 Williamsville Rd.
Stockbridge
(413) 298-3579
chesterwood.org

The Clark Art Institute
225 South St.
Williamstown
(413) 459-2303
clarkart.edu

Frelinghuysen Morris House & Studio
92 Hawthorne St.
Lenox
(413) 637-0166
frelinghuysen.org

Hancock Shaker Village
1843 Housatonic St.
Pittsfield
(413) 443-0188
hancockshakervillage.org

**Massachusetts Museum of
Contemporary Art (MASS MoCA)**
4040 Mass MoCA Way
North Adams
(413) 662-2111
massmoca.org

Monument Mountain
State Route 23
Great Barrington
(413) 298-3239
trustees.org

The Mount
2 Plunkett St.
Lenox
(413) 551-5111
edithwharton.org

Mount Greylock
30 Rockwell Rd.
Lanesborough
(413) 499-4262
mass.gov

Naumkeag
5 Prospect Hill
Stockbridge
(413) 298-8138
trustees.org

season lasts for only seven weeks in July and August, the BSO is very much the economic engine for the entire region. Today the Berkshires region is a cultural paradise; artistic, literary, and historic treasures abound throughout the region year-round.

Southern Berkshires

Life in the Southern Berkshires centers on the town of Great Barrington, which lately has become a satellite community for Brooklyn expats. With a history of small-scale farms and handcrafted foods, Great Barrington has become a true foodie destination with a plethora of buzzy restaurants.

trivia

The region was named the Berkshires in 1761 to honor the home county of Royal Governor Sir Francis Bernard.

Get ready for a short, moderate hike with a big payoff at the end. At eighty feet, ***Bish Bash Falls*** (413-528-0330; mass.gov) is a single-drop waterfall that is also the state's highest. It's an easy half-mile woodsy walk down the trail from the parking lot. Once you've glimpsed the falls, if you want to continue, it's just another mile to cross the New York state line and into Taconic State Park. Open sunrise to sunset. The parking lot is located at Falls Road.

At the crossroads of State Route 57, the ***Old Inn on the Green*** (413-229-7924; oldinn.com) dates from 1760 and was once a stagecoach stop. Today the two-story white clapboard building is an inn and restaurant owned and operated by renowned chef Peter Platt and his wife, Meredith Kennard. The romantic dining room features a wood-burning fireplace and white linen–draped tables and is lit entirely by candlelight. Platt's creative and sophisticated three-course prix fixe menu might include parsley and quinoa–crusted cod with braised endive or slow-braised lamb shank with polenta and grilled zucchini. And who could say no to warm bread pudding with bourbon sauce and fresh cream gelato? If you would like the pampering to continue, book a stay at the

TOP ANNUAL EVENTS

APRIL

Baby Animals Festival
Hancock Shaker Village
Pittsfield
(413) 443-0188
hancockshakervillage.org

JULY

Bang on a Can
MASS MoCA
North Adams
(413) 662-2111
massmoca.org

Berkshire Arts Festival
Ski Butternut
Great Barrington
(413) 528-2000
berkshires.org

OCTOBER

Fall Foliage Festival & Parade
North Adams
(413) 499-1600
1berkshire.com

DECEMBER

Stockbridge Main Street at Christmas
Stockbridge
(413) 298-5200
stockbridgechamber.org

inn, which has eleven homey rooms, individually themed and decorated. The inn's address is 134 Huntsville–New Marlborough Road, next to the Meeting House on the New Marlborough Village Green.

Hyper-seasonal, the "eat local" ethos is taken very seriously at *Prairie Whale* (413-528-5050; prariewhale.com). Many of the restaurant's ingredients come straight from owner Mark Firth's nearby eighty-two-acre Monterey Farm. Seasonality is the name of the game here; in the spring find brick chicken plated with dandelion greens; in summer there's tomato soup with Grana Padano cheese and a big handful of fresh basil. The restaurant is located at 178 Main Street in a former bookstore in the center of Great Barrington.

Practically equidistant between Great Barrington and Stockbridge, *Monument Mountain* (413-298-3239; trustees.org) has been a source of inspiration to many. The mountain was the site of a sacred Mohican stone monument as recently as the 1830s, and its name is in recognition of its importance to the Mohican people. This spot has also been a favorite Berkshire hike since the nineteenth century, capturing the imagination of Nathaniel Hawthorne, Herman Melville, and Oliver Wendall Holmes. The easiest way to the top is Mohican Monument Trail—a short, one-and-a-half-mile gradual climb that delivers views of the Housatonic River Valley and the Taconic Mountains. Look for the trailhead along US 7, three and a half miles north of the State Route 23 junction in Great Barrington. The park is open daily dawn to dusk, and there is a parking fee of $6.

It's a short ride south along pretty US 7 to Sheffield. Along the way, turn off at Covered Bridge Lane to see the eye-catching *Upper Sheffield Covered Bridge*. A bridge has spanned this section of the Housatonic River since 1832; the current bridge is a 1999 restoration, and it is open to pedestrians who want to walk across its ninety-three-foot span. Pick up US 7 again, continuing south to *Ashley House* (413-298-3239; trustees.org) at 117 Cooper Hill Road. The large farmhouse was built in 1735 for Colonel John Ashley and his family; it is the oldest still-standing home in the Berkshires. Ashley was one of the most influential men in the region at the time: a large landholder, a lawyer, and a businessman. He was also a slave owner. In 1781 one of his slaves, Mum Bett, brought a lawsuit against him in the county court of appeals, challenging her enslavement. She won her case and her freedom, which helped bring about the abolition of slavery in Massachusetts, in 1783. The home is open for guided tours; check the website for days and times.

The Berkshires are enchantingly lovely in winter; the hills and tiny towns are sugarcoated and sparkling with snow from December through March. Within the ski world, the Berkshires are not well-known among purists, but

Butternut (413-528-2000; skibutternut.com) is fun for a day trip. Although small, Butternut offer most of the same amenities as do the larger resorts in neighboring states—lessons, lifts, and a ski shop, as well as twenty-two trails and snowmaking. Bonus: Butternut has eight lanes of snowtubing, so you can cruise down the mountain without much effort. Just five minutes outside of Great Barrington, Butternut is located at 380 State Road.

Central Berkshires

High culture meets nature in the picture-perfect central Berkshires towns of Lenox and Stockbridge, making either a good choice as a base for exploring the region. Pittsfield looks like a lot of postindustrial Massachusetts manufacturing centers, but there are signs that the town is making a comeback.

Two miles from the center of Lenox, the mansion looming ahead after you turn onto Plunkett Street is *The Mount* (413-551-5111; edithwharton.org), home of novelist Edith Wharton. Wharton was the first woman to win the Pulitzer Prize in fiction for her book *The Age of Innocence*. The Mount is very much an autobiographical house; Wharton had a hand in its construction and later wrote an interior design book, *The Decoration of Houses*, based on the experience. One could say Wharton was a lifestyle influencer. The house is open for guided and self-guided tours daily from 10 a.m. to 5 p.m. Admission is $20 for adults and free for children. There is no charge to explore the estate's extensive wooded grounds and French and Italianate gardens, which are open daily from dawn to dusk.

Miraval Berkshires (413-881-1234; miravalberkshires) is an all-inclusive spa hideaway that combines Northeastern charm with upscale wellness culture. Start your morning with a yoga class followed by a cardio session. The spa is as next-level as the activities; spend the afternoon relaxing in the sauna or by the indoor/outdoor pool. Your stay includes resort credits that can be used for an array of pampering treatments. All meals, snacks, and drinks are included as well. It's like summer camp for adults—you may never want to leave. The resort is on the outskirts of Lenox at 55 Lee Road.

The Bookstore (413-637-3390; bookstoreinlenox.com) has been a Lenox anchor for more than forty years. The carefully curated shop is in Lenox center at 11 Housatonic Street. And if books and wine are your idea of a happy place, you are in luck. Grab a seat at the next-door *Get Lit Wine Bar*, sip, and browse through the latest releases as you lose all sense of time.

A nondescript brick building at 8 Franklin Street is the home of *Haven* (413-637-8948; havencafebakery.com). Haven is a bakery and restaurant that serves as the Lenox community living room, with morning muffins, croissant French toast, and eggs Benedict; lunchtime salads, sandwiches, and burgers; and, at dinner, take-out catering—all with an emphasis on local produce and purveyors.

Tanglewood (617-266-1200; bso.org) is the Boston Symphony Orchestra's summer home in the Berkshires, so it is not exactly under the radar; but many concertgoers are still surprised to learn that the history of the summer music festival has its roots in educating the next generation of classical musicians. It has been estimated that nearly 20 percent of current American symphony orchestra members have been Tanglewood Music Center Fellows. And while during any given summer season, Yo-Yo Ma, John Williams, and James Taylor are the headline acts, numerous TMC Fellow concerts, workshops, and talks take place on campus nearly every day of the festival are open to the public— and free. The Tanglewood season runs from early July through mid-August. The Lenox campus address is 297 West Street.

Down a long drive in the center of Lenox, the *Frelinghuysen Morris House & Studio* simply wows. It is the former residence of George L. K. Morris and his wife, Suzy Frelinghuysen, both prominent abstract Cubist artists during the 1940s and 1950s. The Bauhaus-inspired white stucco and glass block house and studio speaks to the Modernist aesthetic of the time. Inside, visitors will find the couple's furnishings still in place, their own works, and paintings by the couple's better-known friends and colleagues, such as Pablo Picasso. The house is at 92 Hawthorne Street and is open late June through mid-October, Thursday through Sunday, from 10 a.m. to 4 p.m.

Scattered throughout the rolling farmland of the Berkshires are a number of apple orchards that make for a perfect afternoon of wholesome activity. Just twelve minutes from Lenox, two-hundred-acre *Hilltop Orchards* (413-344-6817; hilltoporchards.com) has it all: an orchard, a winery, a cidery, and a farm store. You'll find your perfect fall during their pick-your-own apple season, which generally runs from mid-August to late October. The real draw here is their taproom, open year-round, where you can taste hard cider and wines made from their farm-fresh fermented fruit. Hilltop is on the New York– Massachusetts border in the town of Richmond at 508 Canaan Road and is open daily from 9 a.m. to 5 p.m.

Stockbridge

Daniel Chester French (1850–1931) sculpted the models for many of his most famous works, including his seated statue of Abraham Lincoln for the Lincoln Memorial, at *Chesterwood* (413-298-3579; chesterwood.org), his summer home. His working studio was in New York City; he purchased the Stock-bridge property in 1896 as a retreat from city life and for its view of Monument

Mountain. The estate includes the French family's nine-bedroom home, French's working studio space, formal gardens, and a woodland walk. French was a prolific artist; Chesterwood holds nearly five hundred examples of French's work, including both plaster models and finished bronze and marble sculptures. It's a fascinating look at the creative process of one of America's most highly regarded sculptors. The estate's address is 4 Williamsville Road. Admission is $20 for adults and free for children age thirteen and under.

To say that the **Red Lion Inn** (413-298-5545; redlioninn.com) is iconic is an understatement. Besides being one of the oldest hotels in the country, having first opened its doors to weary stagecoach passengers in 1774, the hotel was immortalized in Norman Rockwell's 1967 painting *Home for Christmas*. The Red Lion is one of the largest hotels in the region with 108 rooms; some are a tad small, but each has its share of antiques and charming country fabrics. In summer, take it all in from one of the inn's front-porch rockers—it's the place to be to watch Main Street's coming and goings. The hotel's address is 30 Main Street.

Just a half mile down the road from the Red Lion, at 5 Prospect Hill, is **Naumkeag** (413-298-8138; trustees.org), a wonderful example of a Gilded Age Berkshire summer cottage. Built in 1886 for New York lawyer Joseph Hodges Choate and his wife, Caroline, the forty-four-room shingle-style hillside home has lovely mountain views and eight acres of gardens. It is open to the public late May through mid-September, Thursday through Monday, from 10 a.m. to 4 p.m. Admission is $20 for adults, $5 for children ages three through twelve.

On Stockbridge's back roads, hidden in the Berkshire foothills, is **Arrowhead** (413-442-1793; berkshirehistory.org), the farm where Herman Melville wrote his best work, including *Moby-Dick*. From the window of Melville's study, Mount Greylock seems close enough to touch, and it is not difficult to imagine the form of a whale in the outline of the hills. Admission is by guided tour; tickets are $16 for adults and free for children eleven and under. The house is the headquarters for the Berkshire Historic Society and is generally open Thursday through Monday; check the website for exact tour times.

Hancock Shaker Village (413-443-0188; hancockshakervillage.org) is the oldest working farm in the Berkshires. This 750-acre farm dates from 1790 and was the site of a Shaker utopian community that numbered as many as three hundred members in the 1830s. The Shakers sold the property in the 1960s, and it has been transformed into a living history museum that includes a complex of twenty preserved historic buildings, farm animals, and extensive gardens, along with hiking and walking trails. The Shakers called this farm "The City of Peace," and it is easy to see why; there is a certain sense of tranquility in the farm's simple dormitories, the tidy vegetable plots, and well-ordered farm buildings. Among the fascinating places to explore is the three-story round stone barn that was built in 1826 for the dairy herd; its ingenious design made it possible for one farmer to feed fifty-two stabled cows easily and efficiently. The Shakers are perhaps best known for their spare, contemporary design aesthetic. Historic craft demonstrations in woodworking, blacksmithing, weaving, and beeswax candle making are scheduled throughout the day. The terrific gift shop is worth a stop—the oval cherrywood boxes are exquisite. Hancock Shaker Village is on the Pittsfield-Hancock town line at 1843 Housatonic Street. The village is open daily April through December from 10 a.m. to 5 p.m. Admission is $20 for adults, free for children twelve and under.

Northern Berkshires

Tucked in the extreme northwest corner of the state, the northern Berkshires are home to the peerless Massachusetts Museum of Contemporary Art (MASS MoCA) in North Adams and the college town of Williamstown, home of Williams College.

Located on the Hoosic River, North Adams is the commonwealth's smallest city; yet this nineteenth-century mill town is home to the largest contemporary art museum in the country. Opened in 1999, the ***Massachusetts Museum of Contemporary Art*** (413-662-2111; massmoca.org), or MASS MoCA, comprises a maze of galleries strung across twenty-six former mill buildings. The museum is particularly known for its daring, large-scale exhibitions. Sol LeWitt's bold, geometric murals are a visitor highlight—get ready to post to Instagram. The campus is in downtown North Adams at 4040 Mass MoCA Way. From the end of May until the middle of October, the museum is open Wednesday through Monday from 10 a.m. to 6 p.m. The rest of the year it is open Wednesday through Monday, 10 a.m. to 5 p.m. Admission is $20 for adults, $8 for children ages six through sixteen.

Just five minutes out of North Adams, State Route 2 East leads to the Mohawk Trail. Tucked away from the side of the road at McAuley Road is ***Natural Bridge State Park*** (413-663-6392; mass.gov). The thirty-foot natural marble bridge is the only one of its kind in North America. How did this place come to be? The marble formation was shaped into a bridge by glacial runoff after the most recent ice age. The site was a marble quarry from 1810 to 1947; from 1950 to 1983 an enterprising Edward Elder operated the site as a roadside curiosity to visitors along the Mohawk Trail. Today the property is maintained as a small state park with a seasonal visitor center that is open daily, dawn to dusk, from late May through mid-October. The round-trip hike is just a half

trivia

mile and, just as it was in the heyday of auto touring, is still a good spot to break up a road trip.

Although located 6.4 miles apart, MASS MoCA and the *Clark Art Institute* (413-459-2303; clarkart.edu) refer to each other as neighbors. The Clark is one of the country's finest small art museums. The gallery that makes the biggest impact on visitors is the Impressionists; the museum has an excellent collection of works by Monet, Degas, and Renoir. Its American gallery is notable too, including important works by Sargent and Homer. The Clark is located in Williamstown at 225 South Street and is open daily from 10 a.m. to 5 p.m. in July and August. September through June, the museum is open Tuesday through Sunday from 10 a.m. to 5 p.m. Admission is $20 for adults, free for those age twenty-one and under.

Wandering the back roads of Massachusetts, you quickly realize that there is no shortage of historic house museums in the commonwealth. The *Susan B. Anthony Birthplace Museum* (413-743-7121; susanbanthonybirthplace.com) is a good one; it tells the story of social reformer Susan B. Anthony, who was born in this Federal-style house in 1820 and lived here until she was seven years old. The museum's exhibits celebrate Anthony's work and humanitarian legacy as a leader in the temperance, abolitionist, and women's rights movements. The house is located at 67 East Road. Hours are Thursday through day from 10 a.m. to 4 p.m. Admission is $6 for adults, $3 for children. The house is open for self-guided tours, but try to time your visit to catch the regularly scheduled one-hour tours; the guides offer excellent insight into Anthony's life and times.

At 3,491 feet, *Mount Greylock* (413-499-4262; mass.gov) is the state's highest peak. The auto road is an easy two-mile drive that snakes up through the state park. For hikers, the Cheshire Harbor Trail is a 6.2-mile round-trip up and back hike to the summit. Either way, the prize at the top is the same: commanding views over Vermont, Massachusetts, New Hampshire, New York, and even Connecticut that are especially gorgeous in the fall. Check in at the visitor center in the town of Lanesborough at 30 Rockwell Road. The auto road is open from mid-May through November. *Bascom Lodge* (413-743-1591; bas comlodge.net) is a bit of a legend for Appalachian Trail thru-hikers. The rustic stone-and-wood lodge at the summit offers a mix of private and bunk room overnight accommodations as well as a restaurant serving hearty breakfasts, lunches, and dinners.

More than sixty years on, the ***Williamstown Theatre Festival*** (413-458-3252; wtfestival.org) is still one of the country's best summer stages. Williamstown has always attracted first-class talent. Recent past performers have included Jesse Tyler Ferguson, Audra McDonald, Matthew Broderick, and Taylor Schilling. Of late, there has been a rethink in programing to include promising works from Black, Asian American, and Latinx artists. The festival takes place on the campus of Williams College, 1000 Main Street, at the junction of State Route 2 and US 7.

Places to Stay in the Berkshires

GREAT BARRINGTON

The Barrington
281 Main St.
(413) 528-6159
thebarringtongb.com

Granville House
98 Division St.
(201) 450-1824
granvillehouseinn.com

**Lantern House Motel
Great Barrington**
256 Stockbridge Rd.
(413) 528-2350
thelanternhousemotel.com

HANCOCK

Jiminy Peak Mountain Resort
37 Corey Rd.
(413) 738-5500
jiminypeak.com

LENOX

Garden Gables Inn
135 Main St.
(413) 637-0193
gardengablesinn.com

Gateways Inn
51 Walker St.
(413) 637-2532
gatewaysinn.com

Hampton Terrace Inn
91 Walker St.
(413) 637-1773
hamptonterraceinn.com

NORTH ADAMS

Blackinton Manor
1391 Massachusetts Ave.
(413) 663-5795
blackintonmanor.com

Hotel Downstreet
40 Main St.
(413) 663-6500
hoteldownstreet.com

Porches Inn
231 River St.
(413) 664-0400
porches.com

Tourists
915 State Rd.
(413) 347-4995
touristswelcome.com

PITTSFIELD

Hotel on North
297 North St.
(413) 358-4440
hotelonnorth.com

RICHMOND

The Inn at Kenmore Hall
1385 State Rd.
(413) 698-8100
innatkenmorehall.com

WILLIAMSTOWN

Guesthouse at Field Farm
554 Sloan Rd.
(413) 458-3135
fieldfarm.org

Williams Inn
101 Spring St.
(413) 458-9371
williamsinn.com

Places to Eat in the Berkshires

ADAMS

Haflinger Haus
17 Commercial St.
(413) 743-2221
haflingerhaus.com
Austrian

GREAT BARRINGTON

Baba Louie's
42/44 Railroad Rd.
(413) 528-8100
babalouiespizza.com
Pizza

Housatonic
Pleasant & Main
1063 Main St.
(413) 274-6303
pleasantandmain.com
American

Moon Cloud
47 Railroad St.
(413) 429-1101
mooncloudgb.com
Wine bar

Number Ten
10 Castle St.
(413) 528-5244
numbertengb.com
Steak house

Xicohtencatl
50 Stockbridge Rd.
(413) 528-2002
xicohmexicano.com
Mexican

LENOX

Alta Wine Bar
34 Church St.
(413) 637-0003
altawinebar.com
Mediterranean

Chocolate Springs Café
55 Pittsfield Rd.
(413) 637-9820
chocolatesprings.com
Coffee/ice cream

Nudel
37 Church St.
(413) 551-7183
nudelrestaurant.com
Seasonal farm-to-table

NEW MARLBOROUGH

Cantina 229
229 Huntsville–New
Marlborough Rd.
(413) 229-3276
cantina229.com
Tacos/world cuisine

OTHER ATTRACTIONS

Berkshire Botanical Garden
5 West Stockbridge Rd.
Stockbridge
(413) 298-3926
berkshirebotanical.org

Berkshire Museum
39 South St.
Pittsfield
(413) 443-7171
berkshiremuseum.org

Jacob's Pillow
358 George Carter Rd.
Becket
(413) 243-9919
jacobspillow.org

Norman Rockwell Museum
9 Glendale Rd.
Stockbridge
(413) 298-4100
nrm.org

Shakespeare & Company
70 Kemble St.
Lenox
(413) 637-1199
shakespeare.org

SELECTED CHAMBERS OF COMMERCE & TOURISM BUREAUS

The Berkshires
66 Allen St.
Pittsfield 01201
(413) 499-1600
berkshires.org

Hampshire County Tourism & Visitors Bureau
99 Pleasant St.
Northampton 01060
(413) 584-1900
visithampshirecounty.com

Lenox Chamber Visitor Center
4 Housatonic St.
Lenox 02140
(413) 637-3646
lenox.org

Mohawk Trail
North Adams 01247
(413) 743-8127
mohawktrail.org

Western Mass/Greater Springfield Convention & Visitors Bureau
1441 Main St.
Springfield 01103
(413) 787-1548
explorewesternmass.com

NORTH ADAMS

Jack's Hot Dog Stand
12 Eagle St.
(413) 664-9006
jackshotdogstand.com
Hot dogs/hamburgers

Public Eat & Drink
34 Holden St.
(413) 664-4444
publiceatanddrink.com
Gastropub

PITTSFIELD

BB's Hot Spot
302 Columbus Ave.
(413) 464-9030
bbshotspot.com
Caribbean

Crust Pizza
505 East St.
(413) 464-7977
crustpz.com
Pizza

District Kitchen
40 West St.
(413) 442-0303
district.kitchen
Gastropub

STOCKBRIDGE

Once Upon a Table
36 Main St.
(413) 298-3870
onceuponatable.com
Farm-to-table

Six Depot Roastery & Café
6 Depot St.
(413) 232-0205
sixdepot.com
Café

WEST STOCKBRIDGE

Truc Orient Express
3 Harris St.
(413) 232-4204
Vietnamese

WILLIAMSTOWN

Gramercy Bistro
16 Water St.
(413) 458-6222
gramercybistro.com
Contemporary American

Hot Tomatoes Pizza
100 Water St.
(413) 458-2722
Hottomatoespizza.com
Pizza

Mezze
777 Cold Spring Rd.
(413) 458-0123
mezzerestaurant.com
Contemporary American

Tunnel City Coffee
100 Spring St.
(413) 458-5010
tunnelcitycoffee.com
Café/breakfast

Index

A

Abby Park, 62
Abiel Smith School, 7
Abroad, 89
AC Hotel by Marriott at
    Cleveland Circle, 27
AC Hotel by Marriott
    Worcester, 103
Acorn Street, 6
Adam's National
    Historical Park, 55, 60
Addison Choate, 48
African Meeting House, 7
Afternoon Tea at the
    Boston Public
    Library, 14
A & J King Artisan
    Bakers, 39
Alba, 63
Alden & Harlow, 31
Allen House and
    Amherst Inn, 116
All Saints Way, 11
Alta Wine Bar, 130
American Antiquarian
    Society, 96
America's Hometown
    Thanksgiving
    Celebration, 61
Amherst, 111
Among the Flowers, 82
Anchor In, 86
Antico Forno, 10
Antonio's (New
    Bedford), 62
Antonio's Pizza, 116
An Unlikely Story
    Bookstore & Café, 59
Apatuxet Trading Post
    Museum, 66
Appleton Farms, 35, 43
Aquinnah Cliffs, 89
Aquinnah Lighthouse, 81
Area Four, 31

Armsby Abbey, 104
Arnold Arboretum, 3, 16
Arrowhead, 126
Art Complex Museum,
    57, 60
Art's Dune Tours, 66, 78
Ashley House, 123
AWOL, 86

B

Baba Louie's, 130
Baby Animals
    Festival, 122
Back Bay, 12
Back Door
    Doughnuts, 80
b-Ack Yard BBQ, 88
Bambolina, 51
Bancroft Tower, 96
Bang on a Can, 122
Bar 25, 50
Barcelona Wine Bar, 29
Barn Bowl & Bistro, 88
Barnstable County
    Fair, 68
Barrington, The, 129
Barstow's Dairy Store &
    Bakery, 113
Barstow's Longview
    Farm, 113
Bascom Lodge, 128
Battle Road Trail, 23
Battle Road Trail at
    Minuteman National
    Park, 3
BB's Hot Spot, 131
Beach Plum Inn, 86
Beach Road, 88
Beacon Hill, 6
Beacon Waterfront
    Inn, 61
Beauport Hotel
    Gloucester, 48
Bedford Farms, 32

Beechwood Hotel, 103
Beehive, 28
Behind the Bookstore, 88
Belfry Inn & Bistro, 87
Beneski Museum of
    Natural History,
    107, 112
Berkshire Arts
    Festival, 122
Berkshire Botanical
    Garden, 130
Berkshire Museum, 130
Best Western Adams Inn
    Quincy-Boston, 61
Birch Tree Bread
    Company, 104
Bish Bash Falls, 122
Bistro 63, 116
Black Heritage Trail, 7
Blackinton Manor, 129
Black Sheep Deli, 116
Blackstone River and
    Canal Heritage Park,
    93, 98
Blackstone River
    Valley, 98
Blackstone Valley
    Chamber of
    Commerce, 103
Black Walnut Inn, 116
Black Whale, 62
Bleacher Bar, 15
Bluebird Parker
    Beach, 87
Blue Heron, 117
Blue Hills
    Observatory, 54
Blue Hills
    Reservation, 62
Blue Hills Trailside
    Museum, 54, 60
Bob's Lobster, 50
Bookstore, The, 124
Boston, 3

Boston Children's
   Museum, 31
Boston Harbor Islands,
   3, 9
Boston Park Plaza, 27
Boston Swan Boats, 31
Boston Symphony
   Orchestra, 15
Botanic Garden of Smith
   College, 113
Botanic Garden of Smith
   College, The, 107
Bound Brook Island
   Beach, 77
Bourne, 66
Brassica
   Kitchen+Café, 28
Brattle Book Shop, 8
Brewer's Fork, 28
Brewster, 74
Brewster Book Store, 75
Brewster by the Sea
   Inn, 86
Brewster Flats, 74
Brick Pizzeria
   Napoletana, 63
Bridge of Flowers,
   107, 109
Bright Nights at Forest
   Park, 110
Brimfield Antique
   Fair, 99
Brotherhood
   Nantucket, 88
Brown Jug, 90
BSO at Tanglewood,
   The, 121
B.T.'s Smokehouse, 104
Bully Boy Distillers, 17
Butternut, 124
Buttonwood Park
   Zoo, 62

C
Café Landwer, 28
Café Sushi, 31
Caffe Vittoria, 10

Calvin Coolidge
   Presidential Library,
   107, 115
Cambridge, 18
Cambridge Office for
   Tourism, 32
Candleberry Inn, 86
Canteen, The, 78
Cantina 229, 130
Capeabilities Farm,
   66, 74
Cape Ann Museum,
   35, 40
Cape Ann Whale
   Watch, 49
Cape Cinema, 73
Cape Cod Baseball
   League, 75
Cape Cod Chamber of
   Commerce, 90
Cape Cod Hydrangea
   Fest, 68
Cape Cod Mall, 71
Cape Cod Maritime
   Museum, 71
Cape Cod Museum of
   Art, 89
Cape Cod Museum of
   Natural History, 89
Cape Cod National
   Seashore, 66
Cape Cod Rail Trail,
   66, 73
Cape Cod St. Patrick's
   Day Parade, 68
Cape Poge Wildlife
   Refuge, 83
Caramel French
   Patisserie, 51
Castle Hill on the Crane
   Estate, 49
Cedar Street Grille, 104
Central Berkshires, 124
Champney's Tavern, 109
Chapin Memorial
   Beach, 72
Chappaquiddick, 82

Chappaquiddick
   Ferry, 82
Chappaquiddick
   Island, 66
Chapter House Cape
   Cod, 87
Chatham, 75
Chatham Inn, The, 86
Chatham Kayak, 75
Chatham Motel, The, 86
Chesterwood, 121, 125
Chez Antoine, 88
Chickadee, 28
Children's Museum
   Easton, 62
Chillingsworth, 87
Chinatown Gate, 12
Choate Bridge
   Restaurant, 49
Chocolate Springs
   Café, 130
Christmas by
   Candlelight, 94
Christmas Stroll, 68
Cibo, 89
Cisco Brewers, 89
City Experiences, 37
CK Pearl, 49
Clam Box of Ipswich, 44
Clara Barton
   Birthplace, 97
Clark Art Institute,
   121, 128
Cliff Lodge, 86
C-Market, 13
Cobie's, 74
College Club of
   Boston, 27
Compass Rose Inn, 48
Concord, 24
Concord Museum, 31
Concord's Colonial
   Inn, 28
Cooke's Seafood, 89
Cork & Table, 63
Corner Store, 87

Coskata-Coate Wildlife
Refuge, 85
Craig's Café, 55
Crane Outdoors, 35, 44
Cranfest, 61
Crescent Ridge Farms, 6
CRU Oyster Bar, 88
Crust Pizza, 131
Custom House Maritime
Museum, 45
Cutty's, 31

D
Dairy Joy, 27
Daniel Webster Inn, 87
DeCordova Sculpture
Park & Museum, 3, 25
Deerfield Inn, 108
Del Mar Bar & Bistro, 87
Dennis, 72
Derby Wharf National
Recreational Trail, 38
Destination New
Bedford, 63
Destination Salem, 50
Deuxave, 28
Dexter Grist Mill, 68
Dinosaur Footprints
Reservation, 113
Discover Central
Massachusetts, 103
Discover Gloucester, 50
Discover Quincy, 63
District Kitchen, 131
Dorchester Brewing
Company, 17
Drumlin Farm, 26
Dumpling Café, 13
Dunbar House Tea
Room, The, 69

E
East Beach, 83
Eastern State Exposition
(The Big E), 110
Eben House, 86
Ecotarium, 103

Edgartown Harbor
Light, 82
Edward Gorey House,
66, 72
80 Thoreau, 32
Eliot Hotel, 27
Ellery Hotel, The, 116
El Pelon Taqueria, 28
Emerson Inn, 48
Emily Dickinson House,
107, 112
Endless Coast, 87
English Garden Bed &
Breakfast, An, 86
Eric Carle Museum of
Picture Book Art,
107, 112
Essex, 42
Essex Clam Fest, 36
Essex Historical Society
and Shipbuilding
Museum, 43
Essex River Cruises, 43
Essex Street Inn, 48
Eventide, 28

F
Fall Foliage Festival &
Parade, 122
Falmouth, 70
Faneuil Hall, 6
Farmer and the Fork
Café, 101
Fat Cat, 63
Feather & Wedge, 51
Fed at the Langham,
The, 28
Fenway Park, 31
Field Gallery Sculpture
Garden, 81
Finn's Craft Beer Tap
House, 88
Fitchburg Art
Museum, 103
Flynt Center of Early
New England
Life, 108

Forbes House
Museum, 54
Four Seas Ice Cream, 72
Four Sisters Owl
Diner, 50
Franklin County
Chamber of
Commerce, 118
Franklin County Cider
Days, 110
Franklin County Fair, 110
Franklin Park Zoo, 22
Frederick Collection of
Grand Pianos, 102
Frederick Law Olmsted
National Historic
Site, 23
Freedom Trail, 3, 4
Freeman's Grill, 87
Freepoint Hotel
Cambridge, 27
Frelinghuysen Morris
House & Studio,
121, 125
French Cable Station
Museum, 76
Fruitlands, 93
Fruitlands Museum, 100
Fugakyu, 31
Fuller Craft Museum,
59, 60

G
Garden Gables Inn, 129
Garrison Inn Boutique
Hotel, 48
Gateways Inn, 129
George Howell, 6
Get Lit Wine Bar, 124
Giula, 31
Glass Onion, 87
Gloucester, 40
Gloucester Schooner
Festival, 36
Golden Eagle
Restaurant, 111
Goodnight Fatty, 51

Grace Episcopal
Church, 80
Gramercy Bistro, 131
Granville House, 129
Greater Cape Ann
Chamber of
Commerce, 50
Greater Lowell Chamber
of Commerce, 50
Greater Merrimack Valley
Convention & Visitors
Bureau, 32
Great Rock Bight
Preserve, 81
Green Briar Nature
Center & Jam
Kitchen, 69
Green River Festival, 110
Greenway Carousel, 9
Grill 23 & Bar, 28
Gropius House, 26
Guesthouse at Field
Farm, 129

H
Hadley, 113
Hadley Asparagus
Festival, 110
Haflinger Haus, 130
Hail to the Sunrise, 111
Halibut Point State Park,
35, 42
Hampshire County
Tourism & Visitors
Bureau, 118, 131
Hampton Terrace
Inn, 129
Hancock Shaker Village,
121, 126
Handlebar Nantucket, 88
Hanger B, 87
Harbor Lounge, 89
Harborview Inn, 48
Hart House 1640, 49
Harvard Art Museums, 31
Harvard Museum of
Natural History, 3, 22

Harvard Square, 19
Harvard University, 18
Harvest, 31
Haunted Happenings, 36
Haven, 124
Haven, The, 28
Hawthorne Hotel, 48
Heath's Tea Room, 51
Hei La Moon, 13
Henry David Thoreau, 25
Heritage Museum &
Gardens, 67
Herrell's Ice Cream, 114
Hilltop Orchards, 125
Hingham, 56
Historic Deerfield,
107, 108
Holidays by the Sea, 68
Holyoke St. Patrick's Day
Parade, 110
Homestead, 117
Homewood Suites by
Hilton Worcester, 103
Horseneck State Beach
Reservation, 62
Hotel 1620, 61
Hotel 1868, 28
Hotel Downstreet, 129
Hotel Northampton, 116
Hotel on North, 129
Hotel Pippa, 86
Hotel Salem, 48
Hot Tomatoes Pizza, 132
Housatonic, 130
House of Seven
Gables, 49
Hoxie House, 68
Hula Moon, 51
Hull, 56
Hull Lifesaving Museum,
56, 60
Hummarock Beach, 57
Hyannis, 71
Hyannis Whale Watcher
Cruises, 89
Hyve Café, 100

I
Il Casale, 32
Inn at Castle Hill,
The, 44
Inn at Cook Street, 86
Inn at Hastings Park,
24, 28
Inn at Kenmore Hall, 129
Inn at Scituate Harbor,
57, 61
Inner Harbor Ferry, 7
Inn on Boltwood, 116
Inn on Shipyard Park,
The, 61
Institute of
Contemporary Arts, 31
International Volleyball
Hall of Fame, 117
Ipswich, 43
Isabella Stewart Gardner
Museum, 3, 14
Isaiah Jones Homestead
Bed & Breakfast, 87
Ithaki, 49

J
Jack's Hot Dog
Stand, 131
Jacob's Pillow, 130
Jaho, 39
Jake's, 117
James Hook Lobster, 9
Johnathan Young
Windmill, 76
John F. Kennedy
Hyannis Museum, 89
John F. Kennedy
National Historic
Site, 21
Johnny Appleseed Arts &
Cultural Festival, 94
Johnny's Tavern, 117
John Ward House, 38
J.P. Licks, 22

K
Kelleher Rose Garden, 16

Kelley House, 86
Keltic Kitchen, 90
Kitchen Café, 87
Knack, The, 89
Krua Khan Rose, 90

L
L.A. Burdick, 19
Lady Killigrew Café, 111
Langham Hotel
    Boston, 10
Lantern House Motel
    Great Barrington, 129
Larsen's Fish Market, 88
Ledger, 51
Legal Seafoods, 28
Lemon Press, 88
Lenox Chamber Visitor
    Center, 131
Lewis Brothers
    Homemade Ice
    Cream, 89
Lexington, 23
Liberty Hill Inn, 87
Life Alive Organic
    Café, 50
Lighthouse Beach, 82
Lincoln, 25
Liz's Café, Anybody's
    Bar, 90
Lobsta Land, 49
Lobster Pool, 51
Lobster Pot, 90
Longfellow House–
    Washington's
    Headquarters National
    Historic Site, 19
Look Park, 114
Loretta, 50
Lowell, 46
Lowell Folk Festival, 36
Lowell National
    Historical Park, 35, 46
Lowell's Boat Shop,
    35, 46

M
Mac's Seafood, 90
Madaket Mall, 84
Ma France, 32
Magic Wings Butterfly
    Conservatory &
    Gardens, 117
Maguire House, 103
Maison Villatte, 87
Maria Mitchell
    Association, 84
Marion's Pie Shop, 87
Maritime and Irish
    Mossing Museum,
    57, 60
Marshfield Fair, 61
Martha's Vineyard, 79
Martha's Vineyard Bike
    Rentals, 82
Martha's Vineyard
    Chamber of
    Commerce, 90
Martha's Vineyard
    Gingerbread
    Houses, 89
Martin House Inn, 86
Mashpee Wampanoag
    Powwow, 68
Massachusetts Institute of
    Technology (MIT), 18
Massachusetts Museum
    of Contemporary Art,
    121, 127
Maudslay State Park, 45
Meet Boston, 32
Metropolitan Waterworks
    Museum, 3, 18
Metzy's, 50
Mews, The, 90
Mezze, 132
Mida, 28
Mill City BBQ and
    Brew, 50
Millie's, 88
Milton, 52
Mirabeau Inn & Spa, 61
Miraval Berkshires, 124

Mitoi, 83
Moby-Dick, 83, 126
Moby Dick Brewing
    Company, 63
Moby-Dick Marathon, 61
Moby Dick's
    Restaurant, 90
Modern Pastry, 11
Modern Underground, 11
Mohawk Trail, 107,
    108, 131
Mohawk Trail
    Association, 118
Mom and Pops
    Burgers, 76
Monomoy Island
    Excursions, 89
Montague, 111
Montague Book Mill, 111
Monument Mountain,
    121, 123
Moonakis Café, 88
Moon Cloud, 130
Morning Glory Bed and
    Breakfast, 48
Motif No. 1, 41
Mount Auburn Cemetery,
    3, 20
Mount Greylock,
    121, 128
Mount, The, 121, 124
Museum of African
    American History, 3, 7
Museum of Bad Art, 17
Museum of Fine Arts, 31
Museum of Russian
    Icons, 93, 101
Museum of Science, 31
Myers & Chang, 18

N
Naismith Memorial
    Basketball Hall of
    Fame, 117
Nantasket Beach, 62
Nantasket Beach
    Hotel, 61

Nantasket Beach
  Resort, 61
Nantucket, 83
Nantucket Daffodil
  Festival, 68
Nantucket Film
  Festival, 68
Nantucket Inn, 86
Nantucket Shipwreck &
  Lifesaving Museum,
  66, 85
Nantucket Visitors
  Service, 90
Nantucket Whaling
  Museum, 89
Nashoba Brook
  Bakery, 25
Natural Bridge State
  Park, 127
Naumkeag, 121, 126
Neptune Oyster, 10
New Bedford, 58
New Bedford Harbor
  Hotel, 61
New Bedford Whaling
  Museum, 59
New Bedford Whaling
  National Historic
  Park, 59
Newburyport, 44
Newburyport Yankee
  Homecoming, 36
Newcomb Farms
  Restaurant, 62
New England
  Aquarium, 31
New England Botanic
  Garden at Tower Hill,
  93, 101
New England Holocaust
  Memorial, 6
New England Quilt
  Museum, 47
Nickerson State Park,
  66, 74
Nobnocket Boutique
  Inn, 86

Nor'East Beer Garden, 90
Norman Rockwell
  Museum, 130
Northampton, 113
Northampton
  Bicycle, 114
Northampton
  Brewery, 117
North Bridge Inn, 28
Northern Berkshires, 127
Northey Street House
  Bed and Breakfast, 48
Northfield Mountain
  Recreation and
  Environmental
  Center, 108
North of Boston
  Convention and
  Visitors Bureau, 50
North Quabbin Garlic &
  Arts Festival, 110
Norwottuck Rail
  Trail, 114
Notch Brewing, 17
Novara, 62
Nudel, 130
Number Ten, 130

O

Observation Deck
  at Independence
  Wharf, 9
Off Shore Ale, 88
Oktoberfest, 94
Old Deerfield Fall Craft
  Fair, 110
Olde Salt House, 62
Old Inn on the
  Green, 122
Old Manse Inn, 86
Old Mill Inn, 116
Old Sturbridge Village,
  93, 99
Once Upon a Table, 131
Orange Peel Bakery, 80
Orleans, 76
Osteria Vespa, 117

P

Paddle Boston, 19
Pain D'Avignon, 88
Palmer House Inn, 86
Paper House, 42
Paramount, 28
Parish Café & Bar, 28
Parker River National
  Wildlife Refuge,
  35, 45
Parsonage Inn, 86
Passports Restaurant, 49
Paul and Elizabeth's, 117
PB Boulangerie
  Bistro, 90
Peabody Essex Museum,
  37, 49
Pelham House Resort, 86
Pheasant, The, 87
Pho 88, 50
Picco, 28
Pier 6 Charlestown, 28
Pilgrim Monument
  Provincetown Art
  Museum, 89
Pizza Barbone, 88
Pleasant Bay, 76
Plimoth Patuxet
  Museums, 58
Plymouth, 57
Plymouth Bay Winery, 58
Plymouth Rock, 62
Polar Park, 93, 95
Polly Hill Arboretum, 81
Porches Inn, 129
Port City Sandwich
  Company, 50
Porter Square Hotel, 28
Portuguese Feast of the
  Blessed Sacrament, 61
Prairie Whale, 123
Provincetown Causeway
  Hike, 78
Provincetown Office of
  Tourism, 90
Public Eat & Drink, 131
Publick House, 31, 103

Pulse Café, 117
Punto Urban Art
    Museum, 35, 37
Puppet Lending
    Library, 13
Purgatory Chasm State
    Reservation, 93, 98

Q
Q Restaurant, 13
Quick's Hole
    Taqueria, 88
Quincy, 54
Quincy Market, 6

R
Rami's, 23
Rancatore's, 32
Red Horse Inn, 86
Red Lion Inn, 61, 126
Red's Sandwich Shop, 51
Revere Beach
    International Sand
    Sculpting Festival, 36
Richardson's Candy
    Kitchen, 107
River Bend Visitor
    Center, 98
River Rat Race, 110
Rivers Bend, 49
Rockfish, 88
Rock Harbor, 75
Rockport, 41
Rocky Neck Art
    Colony, 40
Rogers and Brown
    House, 48
Rogers, Fred, 85
Ropes Mansion, 38
Rose Kennedy Greenway
    Park, 12
Row 34, 28
Royall House & Slave
    Quarters, 21
Roy Moore Lobster, 51
Rubato, 55
Russell House Tavern, 32

Rye Tavern Plymouth, 63

S
Sagamore Bridge, 66, 67
Salada Tea Doors, 14
Salem, 37
Salem Cross Inn, 104
Salem Heritage Days, 36
Salem Maritime National
    Historic Site, 49
Salem Waterfront Hotel
    and Suites, 48
Salem Witch Trials
    Memorial, 35, 39
Sally Webster Inn, 48
Salmon Falls Artisan
    Studios, 109
Sal's Place, 90
Salt Island, 41
Sandwich, 67
Sandwich Glass Museum,
    66, 69
Sandwich Inn and
    Suites, 87
Sarma, 32
Saugus Iron Works,
    35, 36
Scargo Pottery, 73
Scargo Tower, 73
Scarlet Oak Tavern, 62
Scituate, 56
Scottish Bakehouse, 88
Sea Coast Inn, 86
Sea Street Café, 88
See Plymouth
    Tourism, 63
Sesuit Harbor Café, 87
Sesuit Harbor House, 86
Shakespeare &
    Company, 130
Shalin Liu Performance
    Center, 41
Shark Center
    Provincetown, 79
Shaw Memorial to the
    54th Regiment, 7

Shea's Riverside Inn &
    Motel, 48
Shelburne Falls Trolley
    Museum, 109
Ships Knees Inn, 86
Shojo, 12
Short & Main, 49
Singing Beach, 40
Six Depot Roastery &
    Café, 131
Six Flags New
    England, 117
Skaket Beach Motel, 86
Skinner State Park,
    107, 113
Skinny House, 12
Sleepy Hollow
    Cemetery, 24
Smith College Museum
    of Art, 114
Smoke Shop, The, 32
Snowy Owl Coffee
    Roasters, 87
Snug, 56
Sofra, 20
Something Natural, 84
Sonesta Select, 48
Southern Berkshires, 121
South Orleans Beach, 76
Spanky's Clam Shack, 88
Spellman Museum of
    Postal History, 27
Spinnaker, 87
Spohr Gardens, 71
Sportello, 28
Springfield, 115
Springfield Jazz & Roots
    Festival, 110
Springfield Museums,
    107, 116
stART on the Street, 94
Steel & Rye, 62
Steps Beach, 83
Sterling Fair, 94
Stockbridge, 125
Stockbridge Main Street
    at Christmas, 122

Stone Crust Pizza, 50
St. Peter's Fiesta, 36
Straitsmouth Island, 42
Student Prince, 117
Sturbridge, 99
Sturbridge Tourist
    Association, 103
Sugar Magnolia's, 49
Sunset Club, 50
Susan B. Anthony
    Birthplace
    Museum, 128
Sweet Cheeks Q, 28
Swift River Museum, 116

T
Table Talk Pie Store, 96
Talise, 49
Tanglewood, 125
Taylor, Marshall
    "Major", 96
Thatcher Island, 41
Theodore's, 117
Thirsty Scholar, 32
Thornton W. Burgess
    Society, 69
Three County Fair, 110
Toro, 29
Tosca, 62
Tougas Family Farm, 101
Tourists, 129
Town Cove Park, 76
Town Meeting Bistro, 24
Townshend, The, 63
Trails & Sails, 36
Treehouse Brewing
    Company, 90
Tree House Lodge, 86
Troquet, 29
Truc Orient Express, 131
Tunnel City Coffee, 132
Turner's Fall
    Fishway, 107
Turners Seafood, 51
Tuscan Sea Grill &
    Bar, 51

U
Uni, 29
United First Parish
    Church, 55
United States Naval
    Shipbuilding
    Museum, 55
Upper Sheffield Covered
    Bridge, 123

V
Vaillancourt Folk Art, 99
Valley Bike, 115
Ventuno, 88
Vida Boutique Inn, 104

W
Wachusett Area Chamber
    of Commerce, 103
Wachusett Mountain, 102
Wachusett Mountain
    State Park, 102
Wachusett Mountain
    State Reservation, 93
Walden Pond, 25
Water Street Kitchen, 88
Wellfleet, 76
Wellfleet Bay Wildlife
    Sanctuary, 77
Wellfleet Drive-In, 77
Wellfleet Oyster Fest, 68
Western Massachusetts/
    Greater Springfield
    Convention & Visitors
    Bureau, 118
Western Mass/
    Greater Springfield
    Convention & Visitors
    Bureau, 131
West Harwich, 87
Whalehouse, 61
Whistler House Museum
    of Art, 47
Whistler, James
    McNeill, 47

White Farms Ice
    Cream, 44
Willard Clock
    Museum, 98
Williams Inn, 130
Williamstown Theatre
    Festival, 129
Woodman's of Essex, 49
Wood Neck Beach, 70
Woods Hill Table, 32
Woods Hole
    Oceanographic
    Institute, 70
Woods Hole
    Oceanographic
    Institute, The, 66
Wood's Seafood, 58
Worcester, 93
Worcester Art
    Museum, 103
Worcester Historical
    Museum, 93, 95
Worcester Public Market,
    93, 97
World's End, 56, 60

X
Xicohtencatl, 130

Y
Yankee Candle
    Village, 117
Yarmouth, 72
Yarmouth Seaside
    Festival, 68
Yiddish Book
    Center, 112
Yidstock: Festival of New
    Yiddish Music, 110
Yolqueria, 90
Young's Seafood
    Shack, 75

Z
Zoar Outdoors, 110